Frontispiece: First line of the Ta-hsueh with Chu Hsi's commentary. Photographed from the 1447 edition of the Ssu-shu chi-chu. Courtesy of the Gest Oriental Library and East Asian Collections, Princeton University.

Chu Hsi and the *Ta-hsueh*

HARVARD EAST ASIAN MONOGRAPHS

118

Chu Hsi

and the *Ta-hsueh*

Neo-Confucian

Reflection

on the

Confucian

Canon

Daniel K. Gardner

Published by

Council on East Asian Studies

Harvard University

and distributed by

Harvard University Press

Cambridge (Massachusetts)

and London

1986

The Council on East Asian Studies at Harvard University publishes a monograph series and, through the Fairbank Center for East Asian Research and the Reischauer Institute of Japanese Studies, administers research projects designed to further scholarly understanding of China, Japan, Korea, Vietnam, Inner Asia, and adjacent areas.

Library of Congress Cataloging-in-Publication Data

Gardner, Daniel K., 1950–
   Chu Hsi and the Ta-hsueh.

   (Harvard East Asian monographs ; 118)
   Bibliography: p.
   Includes index.
   1. Ta hsüeh.   2. Chu, Hsi, 1130–1200—Knowledge—
Philosophy, Confucian.   3. Neo-Confucianism.   I. Title.
II. Series.
PL2472.Z7G37   1986   181'.09512   85–21316
ISBN 0–674–13065–0

To my Parents
MATILDA AND JERRY GARDNER

Acknowledgments

This book has taken shape over many years, benefiting greatly from the good advice and common sense of numerous people. Stephen Owen and Benjamin I. Schwartz of Harvard University and Willard J. Peterson of Princeton University have read various drafts of the work, always cheerfully, always critically. Francis W. Cleaves and Lien-sheng Yang of Harvard University and Ruby Lam of Wellesley College have given generously of their time in reading over translations of particularly perplexing passages. Most of all, I would like to express my thanks to Cynthia J. Brokaw of Vanderbilt University, who has listened patiently. Her criticism has been unrelenting, uncompromising, and invariably penetrating; she has pushed me farther than I would have gone on my own. If readers find this book useful in some small way or other, it will be, then, thanks largely to the help of all these people.

Finally, I must acknowledge my good fortune of having had access to the wonderful resources of the Harvard-Yenching Library, first as a graduate student at Harvard University, then as an instructor at Smith College. It would be difficult to imagine a more professional or congenial staff of librarians. They helped to make what was often tedious bibliographic work as painless as possible. Their good spirits were truly infectious.

Portions of Chapters 3 and 4 originally appeared in "Chu Hsi's Reading of the *Ta-hsüeh:* A Neo Confucian's Quest for Truth," *Journal of Chinese Philosophy* 10.3, and are reprinted here with the permission of the Editor.

Contents

Chu Hsi and the *Ta-hsueh*

Introduction

From the Han dynasty through the early years of the present century, Confucians, looking for inspiration and guidance, would turn to the texts of the Confucian canon. The formation of that canon began in the Han dynasty, during the reign of Emperor Wu (r. 140–87 B.C.), and was not complete until almost 1,200 years later, by which time the original five texts of the Han canon had grown to thirteen. It was thought that these texts, the so-called Thirteen Classics, contained the essential teachings of Confucian doctrine. Reading them was not simply an obligation to be fulfilled; it was a way of engaging in discourse with the revered sages and worthies of the past, and thus coming to a better understanding of the Confucian heritage. Readers often recorded their responses to the words of the sages in commentary, which they would arrange interlinearly in the classical texts. This commentary on the canon became the principal mode of philosophical expression among followers of the Confucian Way.

Today we can read a Classic from the Confucian canon in a variety of ways. For example, we might try to reconstruct precisely what the author of the text had intended. Through extensive philological investigation we would attempt to discover the possible usages and meanings of the characters in the text at the time of its composition. Of course, reconstructing what the author had meant to say is not the same as reconstructing what the text might have meant to generations of Chinese literati reading it. Or, we might take an ahistorical, philosophical approach to the text. In this approach we would search for the reading of the text most convincing to us: what do the characters really seem to be saying? Although some might assume that such a reading of the text is what the author must have intended or is how most Chinese would likely have read it, the purpose of this approach is not principally to uncover the author's meaning or how the subsequent Confucian tradition understood the work.

Then there is the approach that a historian might take and that I have taken in this book. However curious about what the author of the Classic had intended, the historian nonetheless would not concentrate on recovering the original meaning of the work. Nor would he be primarily interested in arriving at a reading of the text that he finds personally satisfying. Rather, his task would be to understand the text as the Chinese themselves at a given time understood it, whether that understanding be convincing to him or not. He would tend to rely on the commentaries and interpretive writings produced over the centuries by Confucian scholars. The historian might choose not to criticize or excuse those readings of the text proposed by the commentaries and other writings that he finds philologically or philosophically inaccurate; for, above all, he is concerned with demonstrating how the text was read and why it may have been read that way, not with whether it should have been read that way.

All these approaches to the canon may be legitimate, but they serve different purposes. The historical approach described last seeks to demonstrate, at least implicitly, the dynamism of the Confucian tradition in China's past. Fundamental to the approach is the belief that Confucian texts were understood differently from period to period and person to person in much the way the Old and New Testaments were in the Christian West. Confucianism was no more an unchanging monolith than was Christianity; just as Aquinas's reflection on texts central to the Christian tradition differed from that of Augustine, so Chu Hsi's (1130–1200) reflection on the Confucian canon differed from that of Cheng Hsuan (127–200). And just as Aquinas's reflection on Christian scripture contributed to his innovative understanding of Christianity, so Chu Hsi's reflection on the canon led to an understanding of Confucianism that would have been all but incomprehensible to a Confucian of the Han dynasty.

The transformed Confucianism preached by Chu Hsi and others beginning in the Sung period has been the subject in recent years of numerous essays, dissertations, monographs, and books.[1] But, strangely, little attention has been given to the relationship between this Confucianism, referred to in the

West as Neo-Confucianism, and the Confucian canon. Such neglect unfortunately encourages the view, espoused as early as the Sung by those inimical to the Neo-Confucian school, that Neo-Confucian teachings were generated almost entirely independently of the Confucian canonical tradition and, indeed, perhaps were more genuinely Buddhistic than Confucian. At the heart of this book is the firm conviction, meant to redress past neglect, that Neo-Confucians of the Sung felt a deep reverence toward the canon and drew inspiration from it.

Of all the Neo-Confucians, none is more closely associated with the canon than Chu Hsi. Chu spent his entire life immersed in study of the Classics, producing volumes of commentaries and interpretive writings on them. However, Chu was not equally interested in each of the Thirteen Classics; certain texts seem to have been more appealing to him than others and so commanded more of his attention. The *Lun-yü* (Analects), the *Meng-tzu* (Mencius), and two chapters from the *Li chi* (Book of rites), the *Ta-hsueh* (Greater learning) and the *Chung-yung* (Doctrine of the mean) especially preoccupied Chu, for he believed that they embodied the essence of the Way. He comments: "If we wish principle (*li*) to be simple and easy to appreciate, concise and easy to grasp, there is nothing better than the *Ta-hsueh*, the *Lun-yü*, the *Meng-tzu*, and the *Chung-yung*."[2] Chu's untiring commitment to these four texts is obvious from a letter written late in his life:

> I have expended a lifetime of effort on the *Lun-yü*, the *Meng-tzu*, the *Ta-hsueh*, and the *Chung-yung* and have nearly perfected my explanations of them. And yet, reading through them recently, I found that one or two large sections still contained errors. I have since been altering them continuously. Sometimes immediately after making an emendation I find still another flaw. From this point of view, reading my own work is no easy matter.[3]

In 1190, having studied them for more than fifty years and written commentaries on them for nearly thirty, Chu Hsi published the *Ta-hsueh*, the *Lun-yü*, the *Meng-tzu*, and the *Chung-yung* as a collection entitled *Ssu-tzu*, the Four Masters. Never before had these four relatively brief works circulated together. In Chu's mind, they constituted a coherent statement of Confucian doctrine. For centuries the Five Classics—the *I ching* (*Book of changes*), the *Shih ching* (*Book of poetry*), the *Shu ching* (*Book of history*), the *Li chi,* and the *Ch'un-ch'iu* (*Spring and Autumn annals*)—had been regarded as the central texts in the Confucian tradition; but Chu, convinced that Confucian principles were more accessible in the Four Masters, urged his disciples to focus on those texts instead. The Confucian tradition would never be the same; for gradually the Four Masters, known commonly since the Yuan era as the *Ssu-shu* or Four Books, displaced the Five Classics as the authoritative texts in the tradition.

Indeed, in 1313, the Yuan government made the Four Books, and Chu Hsi's commentaries on them, the basis of the civil service examinations.[4] For the next six hundred years, any Chinese sitting for any of the government examinations—the provincial examination, the metropolitan examination, or the palace examination—had first to demonstrate a thorough familiarity with each of the Four Books, or, to be more precise, a familiarity with Chu Hsi's understanding of each of the Four Books. Thus, almost all educated Chinese from the Yuan through the Ch'ing dynasties came under the influence of the Four Books; and the understanding that they had of these texts would have followed Chu's reading of them provided in his commentaries. Few works conditioned the post-Sung Chinese intellectual tradition as profoundly as Chu Hsi's exposition of the Four Books.

Of the Four Books, Chu Hsi urged his disciples to master the *Ta-hsueh* first. It was "the gate through which beginning students enter into virtue."[5] Chu referred to the brief text variously as "the foundation," "the outline for learning," "the framework,"[6] and so forth. The *Ta-hsueh* expressed the broad aims of Confucian doctrine—cultivation of the self and the ordering of society—more neatly than any other text in the canon. To Chu's mind it was "the itinerary";[7] it mapped out the general themes of the Confucian school. Once students had fully comprehended it they could continue their travels along the Way confident that they were headed in the right direction. The present study is an attempt to explain how Chu Hsi, and hence later Confucians, read this crucial text. The fully annotated translation of the *Ta-hsueh* that appears here follows, as faithfully as possible, Chu's understanding of the text as revealed in his commentary on the *Ta-hsueh* and in his other writings.

CHAPTER 1

From the Five Classics
to the Four Books:
A Schematic Overview

In 1190, Chu Hsi published an edition of the Four Books—the *Ta-hsueh*, the *Lun-yü*, the *Meng-tzu*, and the *Chung-yung*—known as the *Ssu-tzu*, the *Four Masters*.[1] This was the first time the four texts had ever been published together as a collection; Chu regarded them as the books to be read first, the basic curriculum in a Confucian education. In Chapter 14 of the *Chu-tzu yü-lei* (*Conversations with Chu Hsi, Categorized*), he urges his followers to concentrate on these works:

> . . . Principle is brilliantly clear in the *Ta-hsueh*, the *Chung-yung*, the *Lun-yü*, and the *Meng-tzu*, these four texts. Men simply do not read them. If these texts were understood, any book could be read, any principle could be investigated, any affair could be managed.[2]

And even briefer but more to the point:

> In learning you must start with the *Ta-hsueh*; next read the *Lun-yü*, next the *Meng-tzu*, next the *Chung-yung*.[3]

Chu's high esteem for the Four Books is clear; in his view they are the foundation of the Confucian teachings, even more important than the Five Classics (the *I ching*, the *Shih ching*, the *Shu ching*, the *Li chi*, and the *Ch'un-ch'iu*).

Chu Hsi prescribed a set order in which these four texts were to be read. It would seem that in so doing he hoped to make the learning process more systematic and, hence, simpler:[4]

I want men first to read the *Ta-hsueh* to fix upon the pattern of the Confucian Way; next the *Lun-yü* to establish its foundations; next the *Meng-tzu* to observe its development; next the *Chung-yung* to discover the subtle mysteries of the ancients.[5]

Over and over again we find references in Chu's writings to this suggested reading sequence. In the *Ta-hsueh huo-wen* (Answers to questions on the greater learning),[6] for example, we come across this remark:

It would seem that, if one does not read the *Ta-hsueh* first, there is no way to grasp the outline of learning and thereby to appreciate fully the subtleties of the *Lun-yü* and the *Meng-tzu*. If one does not then read the *Ta-hsueh* with the *Lun-yü* and the *Meng-tzu*, there is no way to understand thoroughly the thread that runs through the three texts and thereby to get at the essence of the *Chung-yung*. Still, if one is not versed in the perfection of the *Chung-yung*, how can one establish the great foundation or adjust the great invariable relations of man, how can one read the world's books or discuss the world's affairs? From this point of view, it is apparent that those who engage in scholarly study must treat the Four Books with some urgency and those who study the Four Books must begin with the *Ta-hsueh*.[7]

To Chu Hsi's mind these texts formed a perfectly cohesive unit, a harmonious whole in which one part had little or no meaning without the other three. Begin with the *Ta-hsueh*, Chu says, then proceed smoothly and logically to the *Lun-yü*, the *Meng-tzu*, and, finally, the *Chung-yung*.

Before the time of Chu Hsi, however, it was the Five Classics that had been the basic works in the Confucian tradition. They had been the first of the so-called Thirteen Classics to be canonized when, in the second century B.C., Emperor Wu (r. 141–87 B.C.) of the Han dynasty established the institution of the *wu-ching po-shih*, the "Erudites of the Five Classics." Emperor Wu had been urged by his ministers to elevate Confucianism and abandon the teachings of Taoism and Legalism; in 141 B.C., he decreed that all non-Confucians, particularly those with Legalist orientations, be dismissed from office[8] and, in 136 B.C., he established positions for Erudites in the five Confucian Classics—the *I ching*, the *Shih ching*, the *Shu ching*, the *Li* (which at that time probably included what we now know as the *I li* (Etiquette and ritual) and most, if not all, of the *Li chi*), and the *Ch'un-ch'iu* (with the *Kung-yang* commentary).[9] The Erudites served as advisers to the Emperor, and, after 124 B.C., also taught students at an Imperial Academy, an institution newly created at the suggestion of Kung-sun Hung (200–121 B.C.). In accordance with Kung-sun Hung's proposal, students at the Academy who performed well, that is, those who showed an expertise in one or more of the Classics, would receive appoint-. ments in the official bureaucracy.[10] This soon became a major means of entering into government service.[11] Hitherto Confucianism, Taoism, and Legalism had been more or less on an equal footing; but, with the establishment of an Imperial Academy where the curriculum and instructors were all Confucian, Confucianism quickly gained a privileged status approaching that of a state orthodoxy, a status that it retained until the present century.[12]

By the mid-ninth century, the original canon of five had grown to twelve, including the *I ching*, the *Shih ching*, the *Shu ching*, the *Li chi* and its two companion ritual texts the *I li* and the *Chou li* (Rituals of the Chou), the *Ch'un-ch'iu* (with the *Tso chuan* commentary) and its two other commentaries the *Kung-yang chuan* and the *Ku-liang chuan*, the *Lun-yü*, the *Hsiao ching* (Classic of filial piety), and the *Erh-ya;* toward the end of the eleventh century the *Meng-tzu* was finally added.[13] Throughout this long process of canonization, however, the Five Classics remained the central and most important texts in the Confucian tradition. Indeed, many of the works canonized after the Han were simply commentaries and companion volumes to texts in the Five Classics.

Although the canonization process continued after the fall of the Han, from the late Han through the T'ang the Confucian Classics stimulated less interest than they once had. Neo-Taoism and, even more so, Buddhism, which had been introduced from India through Central Asia, had caught the fancy of the Chinese literati because of their timely concern with personal salvation and cosmological questions. The political chaos and social upheaval that prevailed throughout China from the second to the sixth century may have enhanced the appeal of these teachings. Broad ontological and metaphysical issues had never been at the heart of traditional Confucianism, and, when it concerned itself with such questions, they were primarily as an adjunct to and support for Confucianism's overriding concern for ethics and a public moral philosophy. Thus, when ontological and metaphysical issues were raised by Neo-Taoism and Buddhism, Confucianism did not respond. The influence of Confucianism declined dramatically and classical studies in turn suffered. Although the canonical works, particularly the Five Classics, were still read and recognized as the fundamental texts in the tradition, studies of them were for the most part uninspired and pedestrian, limited almost entirely to matters of a strictly philological nature.

The Sung period is remarkable for the renewed fervor with which Confucian scholars approached the Classics. Indeed, to be à "Confucian scholar" meant something rather different in the Sung from what it had meant in preceding ages. Almost all the major Sung intellectual figures—men such as Sun Fu (992-1057), Hu Yuan (993-1059), Fan Chung-yen (989-1052), Ou-yang Hsiu (1007-1072), Wang An-shih (1021-1086), Ssu-ma Kuang (1019-1086), Su Tung-p'o (1036-1101), Chang Tsai (1020-1077), the Ch'eng brothers, Hao (1032-1085) and I (1033-1107), and, of course, Chu Hsi—devoted much of their lives to study of the Confucian texts. To their minds there was no question that the canon was the receptacle of the truth; the problem was that it had to be properly interpreted before that truth could be discovered. In relying too heavily on traditional commentaries that often obscured the true message of the Classics, scholars since the Han had failed to grasp the essential meaning of the texts. Now in the Sung they proposed to go back to the bare text, with a more critical mind to finding the truth than had Confucian scholars of previous centuries. This task became something of a mission.[14] With the collapse of the centralized and powerful T'ang empire fresh in their minds, with nomads encroaching on their territory to the north, and with the "foreign" doctrine of Buddhism continuing to usurp the position once held by an indigenous Confucianism, Chinese of the Sung were fiercely dedicated to the creation of a strong, essentially Confucian order, and were convinced that the principles in these ancient Classics could provide the basis for such an order.

In the early Sung, literati intensively studied and commented upon the entire canon of thirteen, giving particular attention to the original five.

But, in the mid-Sung, their focus began to change. They singled out certain texts from among the thirteen: the *Lun-yü* and the *Meng-tzu* (two of the Thirteen Classics) together with the *Ta-hsueh* and the *Chung-yung* (two chapters from the *Li chi*) now found a wide and enthusiastic readership among the Confucian elite. By the late Sung, these four books had come to be regarded as of fundamental importance; and, in 1313, under Yuan rule, they were officially recognized as the basic texts for the civil service examinations. [15] They remained so for the next six hundred years, until the abolition of the examination system in the early years of this century.

THE DEVELOPMENT OF CLASSICAL STUDIES DURING THE SUNG

In the Sung, as in no other dynasty since the Han, the intellectual concerns of the most influential thinkers were expressed principally in their studies of the Confucian Classics—that is, both in commentaries and interpretive writings on specific canonical texts, and in philosophic works based on readings of the Classics. In order to appreciate Sung intellectual history, therefore, it is necessary to understand in rough outline the development of classical studies in the Sung.

Three general approaches were taken in studies of the Classics during the Sung. I shall call them, for lack of better, more precise terms, the "critical," the "programmatic," and the "philosophical" approaches. The "critical" approach sought to determine the authenticity, authorship, or reliability of a classical text or its commentaries. The "programmatic" approach focused on ancient institutions, systems, or moral values described in a classical text and argued for their applicability to the current situation. The "philosophical" approach saw in the Classic an explanation of the cosmos and man's relationship to that cosmos, or of man's inner source of morality. These three categories are not mutually exclusive—that is, one study might combine two, or even all three, approaches—in which case the study is most conveniently typed according to the approach that figures in it most prominently. No single approach belonged exclusively to any one school of thought; rather, it was possible for members of the same school of thought to take different approaches in their studies of the texts. What follows is a broad, tentative sketch of the development of classical studies during the Sung based on a consideration of these three approaches.

The first stage had its beginnings in the mid-T'ang. At that time, scholars began to raise doubts about certain aspects of the classical tradition.[16] For example, Liu Chih-chi (661–721) in his *Shih t'ung* (*Conspectus of history*) questioned the historical soundness of the *Ch'un-ch'iu*, placing the blame for many of its defects on Confucius himself.[17] Half a century later, Tan Chu (725–770) and Chao K'uang (8th century) argued that, in reading the *Ch'un-ch'iu*, one should not adhere slavishly to any of the three officially accepted commentaries—the *Tso chuan*, the *Kung-yang chuan*, and the *Ku-liang chuan*—a proposal contrary to scholarly custom of the time. (Chao K'uang even went so far as to reject the traditional attribution of the authorship of the *Tso* commentary to Tso Ch'iu-ming.) The works by Tan and Chao on the *Ch'un-ch'iu* drew freely on all three of the commentaries, while also boldly asserting independent interpretations of the Classic.[18]

The critical approach taken by Tan and Chao had a powerful impact on classicists of the early Northern Sung (960–1127). Sun Fu, Liu Ch'ang (1019–1068), and Hu An-kuo (1074–1138), in studies of the *Ch'un-ch'iu* that reject earlier, traditional interpretations of the Classic, owe a heavy debt to the works of their T'ang predecessors.[19] The critical and independent spirit exhibited in the studies of T'ang and early-Sung *Ch'un-ch'iu* scholars soon spread to studies of other Classics; the authorship, dating, and reliability of all the classical texts and their official commentaries came under close examination. The growth of this critical attitude toward the canon is noted by Lu Yu (1125–1209), a near-contemporary observer:

> Since the Ch'ing-li reign [1041–1048], Confucians have elucidated the meaning of the Classics; in this they are unequaled by men of earlier ages. Yet, they have dismissed the "Hsi-tz'u" (Great appendix of the Book of changes), slandered the *Chou li*, doubted the *Meng-tzu*, ridiculed the "Yin cheng" (The punitive expedition of Yin) and "Ku ming" (The testamentary charge) chapters of the *Shu ching*, and rejected the prefaces to the *Shih ching*. They do not find it difficult to criticize the Classics, how much less the commentaries.[20]

Though Lu Yu is clearly not sympathetic to the critical attitude being displayed toward the canonical texts, his comment testifies strongly to the importance during the early Sung of the critical approach in classical studies.

In the second stage, we find the continuation of this critical approach and the development of the programmatic approach. Hu Yuan and Sun Fu, both teachers in private academies, maintained the critical attitude of the first stage, arguing that traditional commentaries should be disregarded in interpreting the canonical works. But, more significantly, they also began to develop the programmatic approach in their studies, looking to the classical texts for programs of moral and political reform. They viewed the canon as a guide to ethical life and a source of solutions to current problems of statecraft; studying it meant more to them than studying what was necessary to pass the civil service examinations. Their patron, the man responsible for bringing them to the capital to lecture at the National University, Fan Chung-yen, was also well versed in all of the Classics. In Fan we find for the first time in the Sung a man actively involved in government who, like Hu and Sun, emphasized the importance of the Classics to affairs of state.[21] Thus, with Hu and Sun in the academies, and Fan at court, both private scholars and public officials began to regard the Classics differently; no longer were they merely texts to be memorized for the examination as they had been for most literati during the T'ang, but rather books to be critically studied and pondered as a means of discovering unchanging moral truths and sound political principles, which would hold even in the Sung.

The third stage of classical studies was marked by an even greater diversity. With the second- and third-generation scholars of the Sung, there was more activity and complexity in studies of the classical texts. The critical and programmatic approaches were now joined by the philosophical, with the critical and programmatic clearly predominating, as evidenced by many works of the major scholars of the day, including Ou-yang Hsiu, Su Tung-p'o, Ssu-ma Kuang, and Wang An-shih. Examples of the critical approach may be found in Ou-yang Hsiu's *Chou i t'ung-tzu wen* (Questions of a youngster on the Book of changes), where Ou-yang argues that the "ten wings" (*shih-i*) of the *I ching* were not written by Confucius, nor in fact even by a single author;[22] and in Su Tung-p'o's *Shu chuan* (Commentary on the Book of history), where the historical accuracy of the *Shu ching* is questioned, often on the grounds that accounts of certain events are contradicted by information in the *Shih chi* (Records of the grand historian) and the *Tso chuan*.[23] As for the programmatic approach, the most striking and well-known example is Wang An-shih's *Chou li hsin-i* (A new understanding of the rituals of the Chou), in which Wang rejects all earlier commentaries on the text and proposes a new interpretation of his own, emphasizing the applicability to conditions in the Sung of Chou institutions outlined in the *Chou li*.[24]

Simultaneous with the burgeoning of the critical and programmatic approaches was the development of the philosophical approach. Chou Tun-i's (1017–1073) *T'ai-chi t'u-shuo* (An explanation of the diagram of the great ultimate) and *T'ung shu* (Explanatory text on the Book of changes)[25] and Shao Yung's (1011–1077) *Huang-chi ching-shih* (Supreme principles governing the world)[26] serve as examples of this approach. Each of these works attempts, with the aid of Taoist-influenced charts and/or numerological calculations, to explain the evolution of the universe and of man's role in it based on an interpretation of the *I ching* (and, in the case of the *T'ung-shu*, of the *Chung-yung* as well).

The third stage then represents growth and variety in classical studies: Confucians with orthodox Confucian goals and little interest in metaphysical speculation examined the ancient texts more critically than ever before, and pointed to the insitutional and moral programs that might be derived from those texts; yet, at the same time, a smaller group of Confucians, stimulated by some Taoist concepts, began to engage in philosophical speculation on the evolution of the universe in terms of the cosmology of the *I ching*.

In the fourth stage, the philosophical approach came to be used almost exclusively. Parallel to a growing interest in Confucian self-cultivation in the late eleventh and early twelfth centuries, philosophical inquiry, stimulated by the study of the Classics, turned to man's inner source of morality and his relationship to the cosmos. Study turned to a general and universal human morality, and no longer was devoted chiefly to morality in the context of historical action. Those Confucian texts that touched on these concerns—the *I ching* and the Four Books—took on new importance. Chang Tsai and the Ch'eng brothers, particularly the younger, I, based their philosophies primarily on these five texts. A reading of Chang's most important philosophical work, the *Cheng-meng* (Correcting youthful ignorance),[27] and of his explanation of the *I ching,* the *I shuo* (Explanatory comments on the Book of changes), reveals the inspiration he drew from the *I ching* and, to a lesser degree, from the *Chung-yung* in developing concepts central to his metaphysics—those of *ch'i, t'ai-hsu,* and *t'ai-ho.* And Ch'eng I, in his influential commentary on the *I ching,* the *I-ch'uan I chuan* (I-ch'uan's commentary on the Book of changes), attempted to give a rational explanation of the moral order of the universe and of all human affairs from a reading of the judgments (*tz'u*) appended to that work's hexagrams.[28] In addition to this interest in the *I ching,* Ch'eng I was deeply devoted to what were to become the Four Books; these were the texts he had his disciples read first, before the Five Classics,[29] and the ones together with the *I ching* that provided the inspiration for his philosophical system centering on principle and the nature of things (*hsing*). From his commentaries on these works, which may be found in the *Ho-nan Ch'eng-shih ching-shuo* (Explanations of the Classics by Messrs. Ch'eng of Honan),[30] and his numerous comments in the *Ho-nan Ch'eng-shih i-shu* (The surviving works of Messrs. Ch'eng of Honan)[31] we may conclude that much of Ch'eng I's teaching took the form of textual explication of these four texts.

We come now to the fifth and final stage, which might be described as the maturation and synthesis of classical studies during the Sung. This was a stage dominated by Chu Hsi, who dedicated his life to the study of the Five Classics and the Four Books. In his commentaries on the Five Classics, he took the critical approach, calling into question many traditional views of the canon.[32] For example, he was the first scholar to argue that the *I li* was originally the rites Classic and the *Li chi* its appended commentary.[33] Stylistic concerns led him to doubt the authenticity of the long-accepted ancient-text (*ku-wen*) version of the *Shang shu,* and of the K'ung An-kuo (2nd century B.C.) commentary and preface to it.[34] But his work on the Four Books was even more significant than that on the Five Classics;[35] he spent years—in fact, almost all of his adult life—writing commentaries and interpretations on the *Ta-hsueh,* the *Lun-yü,* the *Meng-tzu,* and the *Chung-yung.* [36] It is for these philosophical interpretations of the Four Books that Chu Hsi is most famous. And rightly so, for much of his influential Neo-Confucian vision developed out of his reading of these four texts.

Though this is only a rough schematization of the development of classical studies during the Sung, it should be apparent that the Five Classics were studied more intensively in the early years and that the Four Books, together with the *I ching,* were studied more in the later years. But the important question remains: what factors were responsible for bringing the Four Books into prominence at this time? The answer to this question helps to illuminate some of the intellectual concerns of Sung China.

The most important reason for the shift in interest from the Five Classics to the Four Books can perhaps be found in the Confucian reaction to the influence of Buddhism on Chinese thought at the time. Stimulated and challenged over the years by the deep philosophical concerns of the Buddhists, Confucian scholars were compelled to answer new kinds of questions. No longer could they restrict their interests to man's relation to man. They were required to ponder man's relation to the universe, if only to support and sustain their abiding concern with man the social being. This led them to philosophical inquiry more ontological or metaphysical than ever before. A genuine tension developed between Confucianism and Buddhism. On the one hand, Confucians were attracted to the kinds of issues being raised by the Buddhists; for example, their concern for self-perfection was the analogue of the Buddhist belief that all men possess within them a good Buddha-nature requiring nurture. On the other hand, they were hostile to what they perceived as Buddhism's total preoccupation with self-realization and the consequent neglect of familial and societal relationships, relationships fundamental to the Confucian persuasion. Thus, Confucians stressed some ideas found in Buddhist teachings, but at the same time they were eager to reject any suggestion, however slight, that they had been influenced by the foreign doctrine. Indeed, that eagerness to reject such suggestions suggests how threatening they were. In the reading of their own canon they discovered in the *I ching* and the Four Books in particular many principles on which to found their new philosophical inquiry. Whereas the Five Classics illustrated Confucian morality with examples from history, described how one should conduct oneself in certain concrete, objective situations, and prescribed ritualistic practices for maintaining a well-ordered society, the Four Books were concerned primarily with the nature of man, the springs or inner source of his morality, and his relation to the universe. As these kinds of concerns became increasingly vital to the Confucian thinkers of the Sung, it was natural that the four texts should grow in appeal and importance.

Another reason for the increased interest in the Four Books was the reaction of scholar-officials to the bleak political situation of the late Northern and the Southern Sung (1127–1279) periods. With the continuing military threat from the north and, more significantly, with the failure, or what was viewed as the failure, of Wang An-shih's attempt at political and institutional reform, there was a growing sense of futility and power-lessness among many of those associated with the Confucian school. They became increasingly pessimistic about the possibility of effecting immediate reform; the reformist idealism of the early Sung had given way to political disillusionment. Convinced now that the political and social order could not be improved by institutional and legal changes alone, they turned their concerns inward to the process of moral self-perfection.[37] Progress in the "outer" realm of political and economic affairs, they felt, depended on prior progress in the "inner" realm of self-cultivation. For only the truly good man could draw up good reforms; and only the truly good man could make those reforms work effectively in society. Consequently, the prob-lems of human nature and personal moral development became issues of great significance, and the Four Books gradually surpassed the Five Classics in importance.

Third, the growth of the canon from five to thirteen works since the Han period had made mastery of the Confucian tradition increasingly difficult. Moreover, an abundance of often confusing and differing commentaries and subcommentaries had grown up around each of the thirteen texts. There is little doubt that Chu Hsi's decision of 1190 to group the Four Books together and to elevate their status above that of the Five and Thir-teen Classics was based primarily on a deep commitment to the content of texts; Chu, like the Ch'eng brothers before him, felt that the kernels of Confucian teachings could all be found in the Four Books.[38] It is likely, however, that, in making this decision, Chu was also moved by a desire, first expressed by the Ch'eng brothers, to simplify what had become an overly scholastic tradition and to make the Confucian doctrine more accessible to a larger number of people.[39] In fact, reducing the basic curriculum from five of the lengthiest texts in the canon to four of the briefest was a step entirely consistent with Chu Hsi's general philosophy of learning. We find in Chapters 10 and 11 of the *Yü-lei* recurring statements that it is far better to read and reread a limited amount of material to the point of complete familiarity than to diffuse one's efforts over too large a body of texts: "In reading, don't value abundance; value only your familiarity with what you've read."[40] Whatever Chu's intent in reducing the size of the basic curriculum, it was an act that was to have profound influence on the development of Chinese thought. Indeed, Ch'ien Mu (1895–) has suggested that, by paring down the amount of reading required in an elementary Confucian education, Chu Hsi did for Confucianism what the Ch'an sect had done for an overly doctrinal Buddhism.[41]

Of the Four Books, the *Ta-hsueh* was the text that Chu placed first in the students' sequence of study. But, before considering Chu's interest in the *Ta-hsueh*, we should trace the development of the text prior to the twelfth century.

CHAPTER 2

The *Ta-hsueh*
before Chu Hsi

The *Ta-hsueh* was originally a chapter in the *Li chi,* a collection of hetero-
geneous writings on ritual compiled, according to tradition, by Tai Sheng
(fl. 51 B.C.)[1] during the Former Han dynasty. Authorship of the "Ta-hsueh"
chapter, like many other chapters in the collection, still remains a question.
The date of its composition also has yet to be resolved; it is variously
placed between the time of Confucius (551–479 B.C.) and Tai Sheng.
There is, however, a growing consensus among modern scholars that the
chapter dates from no earlier than the Ch'in period (221–206 B.C.) and no
later than the reign of Han Wu-ti (140–87 B.C.).[2]

Prior to the ninth century, the chapter received little attention. In fact,
no study of the "Ta-hsueh" is recorded in any of the bibliographic sections
of the dynastic histories before the Sung. In the Later Han, Cheng Hsuan
did write a commentary on the whole of the *Li chi,* entitled *Li chi chu*
(Commentary on the Book of rites), which became the standard interpretation of the text. In the Chen-kuan reign (627–649) of the T'ang, K'ung
Ying-ta (574–648) and other eminent scholars of the day were ordered by
Emperor T'ai-tsung to bring order to the chaotic state of classical studies;
an abundance of interpretations had grown up around each of the Five
Classics, and it was K'ung's responsibility to read through the various commentaries and to standardize the interpretation of each Classic. The result
was a collection known as the *Wu-ching cheng-i* (Standard commentaries
on the Five Classics);[3] in the *Li chi cheng-i* portion K'ung Ying-ta adopted
as standard the Cheng Hsuan commentary and wrote a subcommentary of
his own, which drew upon the views of scholars of the Six Dynasties and
Sui periods, particularly Huang K'an (488–545) and Hsiung An-sheng (d.

578).[4] Naturally, the "Ta-hsueh" chapter was commented upon and annotated in both the *Li chi chu* and the *Li chi cheng-i*, but no more importance was attached to it than to the other chapters of the *Li chi*.

A more profound appreciation for the "Ta-hsueh" began to develop in the mid-T'ang.[5] Han Yü (768–824),[6] best known for his role in the *ku-wen* movement for literary reform, was the first to give prominence to the chapter. Throughout his lifetime, he strove to reassert the superiority of the "true" Confucian Way over the "false" doctrines of Buddhism and popular Taoism, which, since the fall of the Han, had dominated the intellectual and spiritual life of the Chinese. This is nowhere more clearly seen than in his celebrated essay, "Yuan tao" (An inquiry into the true Way).[7] Here he openly attacks the teachings of Buddhism and Taoism for what he characterizes as their inherent selfishness: their exclusive emphasis on personal salvation leads to the complete neglect of the family and the society. In the face of the popularity of these two teachings, Han Yü resolutely defends Confucianism and upholds its traditional aim, the perfect ordering of the household and the society. At the same time, though, he is anxious to demonstrate that Confucianism, like Buddhism and Taoism, values self-cultivation and so is able to provide spiritual mourishment of the type only the other two doctrines were thought to supply. Indeed, in Confucianism personal cultivation is absolutely necessary if society is to become perfectly ordered. It is in this context that the now-famous passage from the "Ta-hsueh" is quoted for the first time:

"Those of antiquity who wished to manifest their luminous virtue throughout the empire put governing their states well first; wishing to govern their states well, they first established harmony in their households; wishing to establish harmony in their households, they first cultivated themselves; wishing to cultivate themselves, they first set their minds in the right; wishing to set their minds in the right, they first made their thoughts sincere."[8]

He continues:

Thus, in ancient times, what was called "setting the mind in the right" and "making the thoughts sincere" would lead to action. But now [the

Taoists and Buddhists] , seeking to set their minds in order, isolate themselves from the empire, the state, and the family. They destroy the natural principle of human relations so that the son does not regard his father as a father, the minister does not regard his ruler as a ruler, and the people do not attend to their work.[9]

Han Yü ingeniously observes that ideas contained in the "Ta-hsueh," a hitherto ignored chapter in a sacred Confucian text, are relevant both to his argument against the false teachings and to some of the crucial intellectual issues of the day, especially self-realization; he skillfully uses the passage from the "Ta-hsueh" to present a Confucian challenge to Taoist and particularly Buddhist beliefs popular at the time.

The next reference to the "Ta-hsueh" we find is in the writings of a disciple and friend of Han Yü, Li Ao (d. ca. 844).[10] Because the "Ta-hsueh" at this time appears to have been ignored generally by the literati class, one is tempted to assume that it was through Li's acquaintance with Han Yü that he became familiar with the *Li chi* chapter. The piece in which the "Ta-hsueh" is quoted is the "Fu-hsing shu" (On returning to one's true nature).[11] In it, Li Ao draws heavily upon the Confucian canon, particularly the *I ching,* the "Ta-hsueh," and the "Chung-yung" (another chapter in the *Li chi*), to give Confucian or at least partially Confucian answers to the burning philosophical questions of the day.[12] "Fu-hsing shu" is written in three sections: 1) a discussion on *hsing,* "nature," and *ch'ing,* "feelings," in which the nature is described as originally good and pure and the feelings as evil operations which at times obscure the nature; 2) an explanation of the self-cultivation process whereby one is able to return to one's originally good nature; and 3) a short statement on the role of self-exertion in the cultivation process.[13]

It is in the second section that we encounter Li Ao's reference to the "Ta-hsueh." There he explains the original condition of the mind as "that of absence of thought, and of freedom from both movement and quiescence."[14] Indeed, for Li the aim of the self-cultivation process is to return to such a state. Li is asked to clarify:

You speak of the original condition of the mind as that of absence of thought, and of freedom from both movement and quiescence. But is one, then, not to hear the sounds that come one's way or to see the forms of objects?[15]

To which he responds:

Not to see or to hear would mean no longer to be a man. And yet it is possible to see and hear clearly but not be aroused by what is seen or heard. To know everything; to do everything; to be immovable in mind and yet to illumine Heaven and Earth—this is the enlightenment that comes with utter sincerity. The "Ta-hsueh" says, "The extension of knowledge (*chih chih*) lies in *ko wu.*"[16]

And when asked what is meant by this line *chih chih tsai ko wu* from the "Ta-hsueh," he explains:

Wu means *wan-wu*, "the myriad things." *Ko* means *lai*, "to come," *chih*, "to arrive." When things come before one, the mind should clearly understand and distinguish among them, yet at the same time should not be moved by them. This is the "extension of knowledge." This is the completion of knowledge."[17]

After this explanation, Li Ao immediately launches into a paraphrase of the well-known "Ta-hsueh" passage that follows the line just quoted by him and is closely associated with the one quoted by Han Yü in "Yüan tao":

Knowledge being complete, thoughts become sincere; thoughts being sincere, the mind becomes set in the right; the mind being so set, the person becomes cultivated; the person being cultivated, harmony is established in the household; household harmony established, the state becomes well-ordered; the state being well-ordered, the empire becomes tranquil.[18]

He concludes that by this process "one is able to form a trinity with Heaven and Earth."[19]

To be sure, Li's program for self-cultivation is colored with Buddhist overtones. The success of the cultivation efforts hinges on the mind's ability to remain unmoved or unaroused, as in the Buddhist cultivation process. Yet, what ultimately sets Li apart from the Buddhists is his professed concern for bringing order to the society once the personal life has been cultivated. The passage from the "Ta-hsueh" is central to his essay: it stresses the importance of what Li interprets as a Buddhist-like process of self-perfection, but, at the same time, with its emphasis on ordering the society, it reminds the reader of his traditional Confucian responsibilities. What is also significant here is that Li Ao singles out the line *chih chih tsai ko wu* for discussion. In "Yuan tao" Han Yü had omitted these first two steps of the so-called "eight steps" of the "Ta-hsueh." But, after Li Ao, this line would remain central to the concerns of all schools of Neo-Confucianism.

In the Sung period, interest in the "Ta-hsueh" increased. Indeed, it even received imperial sponsorship of a sort, for, in the T'ien-sheng era (1023–1032), Emperor Jen-tsung began to confer it upon successful *chin-shih* candidates. In the *Yü-hai,* [20] Wang Ying-lin (1223–1296) includes a section entitled "T'ien-sheng tz'u chin-shih 'Ta-hsueh' p'ien" (The conferment of the "Ta-hsueh" chapter upon *chin-shih* in the T'ien-sheng period), which begins:

> On the *ping-hsu* day of the 4th month of the 8th year of the T'ien-sheng period [8 May 1030] *chin-shih* Wang Kung-ch'en [and others] were honored with a banquet at Ch'iung-lin Gardens. [21] [The Emperor] sent a messenger to confer upon them one scroll apiece of the "Ta-hsueh" chapter. Thereafter the "Ju-hsing" chapter, the "Chung-yung" chapter, or the "Ta-hsueh" chapter [of the *Li chi*] was always conferred upon those successful in the palace examination. [22]

This information is corroborated by other sources, including the *Sung hui-yao chi-kao* (Draft of the important documents of the Sung): [23]

> In the T'ien-sheng period of Jen-tsung . . . the 8th year, 4th month . . . 4th day [8 May 1030] the "Ta-hsueh" chapter was conferred upon [each] newly successful *chin-shih.* From this time on, the "Ta-hsueh" was conferred alternately with the "Chung-yung"; this became common practice. [24]

We can reasonably assume that, by the early Sung, the "Ta-hsueh" had become a chapter familiar to literati and that one of them in attendance at the court had brought it to the attention of the Emperor. Unfortunately, none of the sources from the period reveals the name or names of the individuals responsible for imperial authorization. We can be certain, however, that recognition of the chapter by Jen-tsung did gain for it a much broader readership among the scholar-official class than it had previously had.

Numerous essays and memorials citing the "Ta-hsueh" by literati of the time attest to its rising popularity. From Shen-tsung's reign (1068–1085) through the early part of Che-tsung's reign (1086–1100) in particular, the writings of such men as Tseng Kung (1019–1083), Ssu-ma Kuang, Lü Kung-chu (1018–1089), and Fan Tsu-yü (1041–1098) abound with references to the chapter.[25] These writings describe the Way of the "Ta-hsueh" as the Way of the ancients and exhort the ruler to make the chapter and its precepts the basis of his learning and his actions.

Around this time, Ssu-ma Kuang lifted the "Ta-hsueh" and "Chung-yung" chapters from the *Li chi* text, wrote commentaries on them, and circulated them separately from the Classic as the *Chung-yung Ta-hsueh kuang-i* (General meaning of the doctrine of the mean and the great learning). Ssu-ma's familiarity with the "Ta-hsueh" chapter and his decision to write a commentary on it stemmed no doubt from Jen-tsung's conferment policy; Ssu-ma had passed his *chin-shih* examination in 1038, a year in which the "Ta-hsueh" was bestowed upon all successful candidates by the Emperor.[26] Unfortunately, the *Chung-yung Ta-hsueh kuang-i* is no longer extant, so we are unable to know precisely what type of commentary it was.[27]

In Ssu-ma's collected works, however, there is an essay written in 1083 entitled "Chih chih tsai ko wu lun," in which Ssu-ma outlines his interpretation of the line *chih chih tsai ko wu*,[28] discussed earlier by Li Ao. The essay begins:

> Man's nature is such that there is no one who does not love good and hate evil, no one who does not admire right and feel ashamed of wrong. Still, cases of good and right it seems are few and cases of evil and wrong are truly numerous. Why? Man is enticed by things, compelled by things.[29]

Ssu-ma then describes the way in which men's desires are excited by external stimuli and what can be done in the face of such stimuli to keep oneself cultivated and true to one's nature:

Cleave to humanity as your dwelling place and follow righteousness as your path; put humanity and righteousness into practice by "making your thoughts sincere," control them by "setting your mind in the right," and guide them by "cultivating your person." Then can it be that the empire, the state, and the household will not be well ordered? The "Ta-hsueh" says, "Chih chih tsai ko wu." *Ko* is the same as *han*, "to guard against," and the same as *yü*, "to resist." If one is able to guard against external things, one is then able to know the perfect Way. Cheng Hsuan took *ko* to be *lai,* "to come." Perhaps he had not yet fully grasped the meaning intended by the ancients. [30]

In the Han, Cheng Hsuan had said of this line:

Ko means *lai,* "to come." *Wu* is the same as *shih,* "affairs." When one's knowledge of the good is profound, one attracts (*lai*) good things. When one's knowledge of evil is profound, one attracts evil things. In other words, things come to a man according to what he is fond of. [31]

Cheng had explained the character *ko* by *lai,* "to come." Li Ao had followed Cheng's philological explanation of the character but had interpreted the sense of the line completely differently: "When things come before one, the mind should not be moved by them." Ssu-ma Kuang's interpretation of the character *ko* as "to guard against" is the first revision of Cheng and Li's interpretation, "to come." But his general understanding of the line is similar to Li Ao's in at least one important respect: both believe that one should not be misled by external things. [32]

Ssu-ma's contribution to the history of the "Ta-hsueh" then is twofold. He began the tradition of writing commentaries on the *Ta-hsueh* as a separate work. And, following in the steps of Li Ao, he elevated the line *chih chih tsai ko wu* to a position of primary importance in the text.

That the text had achieved a status independent of the *Li chi* by the middle of the eleventh century is evidenced by Chang Tsai's comment:

Scholars—those who put their trust in the written word—should put their trust in the *Lun-yü,* the *Meng-tzu,* the *Shih,* and the *Shu,* for they are free from heterodox principles. Even though each of these texts comes from the hands of many different Confucians, still they contain no passage injurious to what is right. As for the *Chung-yung* and the *Ta-hsueh,* there can be no doubt that they come from the school of Confucius. [33]

Clearly, in Chang's mind the *Ta-hsueh* was no longer simply a chapter in the *Li chi;* it had become associated with the most important works in the Confucian tradition. And, indeed, there are a few references to the *Ta-hsueh* in Chang's collected writings.[34] However, his acknowledgment of the *Ta-hsueh*'s significance notwithstanding, Chang's contribution to the interpretation of the ideas in the text is unimportant.

The Ch'eng brothers, Hao and I, from Honan, did more to improve the status of the *Ta-hsueh* and to interpret it as a systematic work than anyone before the time of Chu Hsi.[35] According to the account of Ch'eng Hao's conduct written by his brother, in teaching his students Ch'eng Hao "proceeded from the 'extension of knowledge' to 'knowing where to come to rest,' and from 'making the thoughts true' to 'bringing tranquility to the empire' "[36]—all ideas from the *Ta-hsueh*. The importance he explicitly attached to the text is clear from a statement of his in the *Ch'eng-shih i-shu:* "The *Ta-hsueh* is a work handed down from Confucius. One must learn from it, then one may be free from error."[37] Ch'eng I echoed his brother's strong sentiments about the value of the text: "As a gateway to virtue there is nothing so good as the *Ta-hsueh;* contemporary scholars owe much to the continued preservation of this text. As for other works, there is nothing to equal the *Lun-yü* and the *Meng-tzu.*"[38] And, even more emphatically: "In cultivating oneself, one must study the sequence outlined in the *Ta-hsueh*. The *Ta-hsueh* is a perfect work of the Sage."[39] Thus, with the Ch'eng brothers the *Ta-hsueh* became required reading for all who aspired to self-perfection; as such, it became the basis of a Neo-Confucian education.

To make it a more systematic work that would be more meaningful to their students, both brothers revised the order of the *Ta-hsueh* text as it had come down to them in the *Li chi*.[40] They were of the opinion that the bamboo slips on which the text had originally been written had become disordered through time and that Tai Sheng's *Li chi* version was in fact not as the Sage had intended it.[41] Their revised versions were tremendously important, for Chu Hsi, in editing and commenting upon what would become the standard edition of the *Ta-hsueh*, the *Ta-hsueh chang-chü* (The greater learning in chapters and verses) drew heavily on them.[42]

Although Ch'eng Hao and Ch'eng I never wrote a traditional line-by-line commentary on the *Ta-hsueh*, their comments on the text appear throughout the *Ho-nan Ch'eng-shih i-shu* and the *Ho-nan Ch'eng-shih wai-shu* (Additional works of Messrs Ch'eng of Honan). Of particular significance are the space and attention given to the terms *chih chih* and *ko wu*; Ch'eng Hao had relatively little to say about them, but Ch'eng I made them central to his whole philosophy. According to him, there is a supreme *li* or "principle" in the universe. Each thing in the universe shares in this principle, which is to say, each thing has a specific manifestation of it:

> All things under heaven can be understood through principle. "If there is a thing there must be a rule." Each thing necessarily has its manifestation of principle.[43]

In Ch'eng I's interpretation, *ko wu* is the means by which one comes to an understanding of principle:

> The extension of knowledge (*chih chih*) lies in *ko wu*. *Ko* means *chih*, "to arrive at," "to reach." *Wu* means *shih*, "affairs." In all affairs there is principle; to arrive at principle is *ko wu*.[44]

One may "arrive at the principle in things or affairs" in any number of ways:

> One way is to read books, elucidating the moral principles in them. Another way is to discuss people and events of the past and present, distinguishing the right from the wrong. Still another way is to deal with the affairs at hand, settling them as they should be settled. All these are ways of probing principle (*ch'iung li*).[45]

Even from this brief passage it is apparent that the purpose of *ko wu* in Ch'eng's philosophy is not the accumulation of knowledge for knowledge's sake. Encyclopedic breadth of knowledge is not what is valued here. Rather, Ch'eng I is concerned chiefly with the knowledge of moral principles in human affairs; it is principle as it is manifested in man's morality that matters most to him. The purpose of "arriving at the principle in things" then is moral self-development:[46]

Someone asked what the first step was in the art of moral cultivation.

There is nothing prior to "setting the mind in the right" and "making the thoughts true." Making the thoughts true lies in the extension of knowledge, and "the extension of knowledge lies in *ko wu.*"[47] *Ko* means *chih,* "to arrive," as in the phrase *tsu-k'ao lai ko,* "the ancestors arrive."[48] In each thing there is a manifestation of principle; it is necessary to pursue principle to the utmost.[49]

It was this general interpretation of the line *chih chih tsai ko wu* that Chu Hsi adopted; and it was with this interpretation that the line and the *Ta-hsueh* text in which it appeared became essential to the Neo-Confucian philosophical tradition.

It now remained for Chu Hsi to standardize the text, add a supplementary chapter to it, write a systematic line-by-line commentary on it, and develop more fully its philosophical significance for Neo-Confucian thought.

Chu Hsi's Work
on the *Ta-hsueh*

In 1189, at the age of sixty,[1] Chu Hsi completed prefaces to the *Ta-hsueh chang-chü* and the *Chung-yung chang-chü* (The doctrine of the mean in chapters and verses). We know from the *Chu-tzu nien-p'u* (Chronological record of Master Chu), written by Wang Mou-hung (1668–1741) in the early Ch'ing period,[2] that Chu Hsi labored long over both of these works before finally appending the prefaces:

> He had done the drafts for these two books long ago but kept altering them from time to time. Being satisfied now in his own mind, he wrote prefaces to them for the first time. For each he also wrote a *Huo-wen*.[3]

Evidence of a deep interest in the *Ta-hsueh* goes back at least twenty-seven years, to 1162, when Hsiao-tsung succeeded to the throne and invited memorials from scholars and officials.[4] In response the thirty-three-year-old Chu Hsi submitted a sealed memorial (*feng-shih*),[5] his first memorial ever, in which he emphasized the importance of ideas found in the *Ta-hsueh* for cultivating the ruler's person and for bringing order to the empire:

> In the learning of the sage emperors and wise kings of antiquity one apprehended the principle in things and extended knowledge in order to probe the transformation of affairs and things. If the meaning and principle of affairs and things that one encounters are illumined in every detail and are clear to one's mind without the slightest obscurity, then naturally one's thoughts will become true and the mind will become set in the right;[6] hence, dealing with the affairs of the empire will be as [simple as] counting one and two and discriminating between black and white. . . . It would seem that "apprehending the principle in things" and "extension of knowledge" is what Yao and Shun called "be discriminating

and undivided," and that "settting the mind in the right" and "making the thoughts true" is what Yao and Shun called "holding fast the Mean."[7] From antiquity on, what was transmitted by the sages and what was manifested in their conduct was nothing more than these things. As for Confucius, he gathered together all that was good but, in advancing, did not acquire the right position and thus did not practice it [i.e., all that was good] in the empire. Therefore, he withdrew and wrote it down in the form of the Six Classics in order to make it known to those of later generations who would rule the empire, the state, and the household. In these [works] he discussed the order of the roots and branches, the beginning and the end, the first and the last. The portion that is particularly detailed and clear may now be found in the book of Tai [Sheng], in the so-called "Ta-hsueh" chapter. Therefore, the Ch'eng-i dignitary (*Ch'eng-i lang*) Ch'eng Hao together with his younger brother the Lecturer of the Ch'ung-cheng Pavilion, (Ch'ung-cheng-tien shuo-shu) Ch'eng I, great Confucians of recent times who truly got at that learning that had not been transmitted since Confucius and Mencius, both considered this chapter to be a work handed down from Confucius and a text that scholars should devote themselves to first; this is indeed an exemplary view. I humbly hope that Your Majestý will renounce old practices, and useless and frivolous writings; put aside those ideas that seem right but are wrong and those that are heterodox; and give your attention to this Classic which has been handed down, search for a true Confucian who profoundly understands its meaning, and place him beside you at court in order to provide advice.[8]

This is the first historical account given by Chu Hsi of the *Ta-hsueh* text; the esteem in which he already holds the work at this early age is quite apparent.

In the following year, at the age of thirty-four, Chu Hsi was summoned to the temporary capital, Lin-an (modern Hangchou), for an audience with the Emperor. At that time, he presented three memorials, one of which continues the theme introduced in the sealed memorial:[9]

I have heard that in the way of greater learning "from the Son of Heaven on down to the commoners, all without exception should regard the cultivation of the person as the root."[10] The way in which harmony is established in the household, the way in which the state becomes well governed, and the way in which the empire becomes tranquil all derive from this root.[11] Thus, one's person cannot be cultivated aimlessly; thorough inquiry into the root depends simply upon apprehending the principle in things in order that one's knowledge may be extended to the utmost.[12] "Apprehending the principle in things" is a term meaning "probing principle".[13] If there is a thing, there must be its particular manifestation of principle. But principle is without physical form and difficult to understand; things have physical traces and so are easy to observe. Therefore, follow a thing in seeking its manifestation of principle; if the manifestation of principle becomes perfectly clear to one's mind, then naturally in dealing with affairs there will not be the slightest mistake. Hence, the thoughts being true and the mind being set in the right, one's person becomes cultivated; as for establishing harmony in the household, governing the state well, and bringing tranquility to the empire, they too rely upon this [process of apprehending the principle in things and extending knowledge]. This is the so-called "way of greater learning." Although the great sages of antiquity were born knowing it, there is not a case of one who did not [continue to] study it. Yao and Shun handed it down—such is the so-called "be discriminating, be undivided, that you may sincerely hold fast the Mean."[14] From that time on, sage passed it on to sage, and each thereby got possession of the empire. When Confucius did not acquire the right position, he committed it to writing in order to make it known to those of later generations who would govern the empire, the state, and the household. Moreover, his disciples together transmitted it and elucidated it further; the way of greater learning indeed can be said to have been well studied. However, since the Ch'in and Han dynasties, this learning has ceased.[15]

As in the earlier memorial, Chu briefly outlines the history of the *Ta-hsueh* text. He argues that the "way of greater learning" described there by Confucius had been the foundation of the sage-emperor's learning in the golden age of antiquity. Since the days of the Ch'in dynasty, however, the "way" had been neglected. Chu Hsi's message in these memorials to the Emperor is clear: the ruler who once again follows that "way" and makes it the basis of his learning will become a true sage-king and bring complete tranquility to the empire.

In a lecture given in Yü-shan district in the province of Chiang-nan in 1194,[16] thirty-one years later, Chu Hsi continues to stress the central importance of the "way of greater learning" in the education of the ancients:

I have heard that in antiquity scholars followed their own standards; contemporary scholars follow the standards of others. Therefore, sages and worthies in teaching others did not have them link together phrases or write literary compositions simply that they might be successful in the examination or acquire rank and emolument.[17] Rather, it was necessary that they apprehend the principle in things, extend their knowledge, make their thoughts true, set their minds in the right, cultivate their persons, and then, by extension, establish harmony in their households and govern their states well in order to bring tranquility to the empire. Only then was their learning what it should be.[18]

Here, it is the scholar, not the emperor, who is admonished to follow the "way of greater learning." In olden times scholars, together with sage-rulers, had followed the "way" and thereby brought about the golden age; implied here, of course, is the idea that, by following the principles set forth in the *Ta-hsueh*, scholars as well as rulers of the Sung could help to bring about another golden age in Chinese history.

Clearly, Chu Hsi had already done much thinking about the *Ta-hsueh* as early as 1162. But it is not clear when exactly he began to commit his reading and interpretation of the text to writing. In a letter from 1167[19] to Hsu Shun-chih (12th century),[20] a young follower of his, Chu Hsi declares:

Recently, my explanation of the *Ta-hsueh* has been revised in a number of places. There were many extremely vulgar points in my earlier work. In general, my ability was not up to it; I just wrote without care. I myself was confused and so confused others—how terribly dreadful![21]

This remark indicates that Chu Hsi had been writing down his thoughts on the *Ta-hsueh* for some time prior to 1167. It seems likely that these writings had circulated, although it is possible that they were simply Chu's notes on the text for use in lecturing. Whether these writings might have constituted a manuscript, in very preliminary form, of the *Chang-chü* remains a question.

We do know definitely, however, that, by 1174, at the age of forty-five, he had completed or nearly completed a draft of the *Ta-hsueh chang-chü*; and this he circulated among trusted friends, seeking suggestions for its improvement. In a letter to Lü Tsu-ch'ien (1137–1181)[22] from 1174[23] he writes:

> I am forwarding to you a copy of the *Chung-yung chang-chü*. (This is a draft so I trust that you will show it to no one.) There is also a *Hsiang-shuo*;[24] it is lengthy so I have not had the time [to complete it]. I will send it to you later. If you see questionable passages, I would be grateful if you would point them out to me. I am also sending the *Ta-hsueh chang-chü;* it too has a *Hsiang-shuo,* which I will send later.[25]

Fifteen years passed from the writing of this letter to the completion of the preface of the *Ta-hsueh chang-chü* in 1189. It is conceivable too, as already noted, that the manuscript mentioned here had been begun much earlier than the year of the letter, possibly earlier than 1167. Thus, prior to 1189, Chu Hsi had already worked on the *Ta-hsueh chang-chü* a minimum of fifteen years.

In 1176 we find Chu already engaged in a revision of his *Chang-chü* manuscript. In a letter[26] to Chang Nan-hsien (1133–1180),[27] he comments:

> As for the *Chung-yung chang-chü* and the *Ta-hsueh chang-chü*, I have . . . revised both of them once through; I will make copies and forward them to you. I am aware, however, that they still contain passages that should be deleted.[28]

There can be little doubt that, during the fifteen-year period from the first mention of a draft to the prefacing of the *Ta-hsueh chang-chü* in 1189, Chu Hsi devoted much of his time and mental energy to improving his understanding of the *Ta-hsueh* text; during this period it would appear that he made numerous revisions of his *Chang-chü* and solicited suggestions for improvements from his most respected colleagues.

The completion of the preface in 1189, however, by no means marked the end of Chu Hsi's work on the *Chang-chü*. Indeed, it is recorded in his *Nien-p'u* that he was still revising Chapter 6 on "making the thoughts true" three days before his death on 23 April 1200.[29] Comments in the *Chu-tzu yü-lei* and letters in the *Hui-an hsien-sheng Chu Wen-kung wen-chi* (Collected literary works of Chu Hsi), many datable to years after 1189, allow us to observe Chu Hsi's continued openness to revision and doubts about his own interpretation of the *Ta-hsueh*. [30] When asked, for example, just a year after writing the preface to the *Chang-chü*, whether his explanation of the *Ta-hsueh* was final or not, Chu responded:

> At the moment I myself would say that it is reliable. I only fear that in a few years I might again deem it unreliable. This is something out of my control. [31]

According to such comments, it would seem that Chu Hsi was not as "satisfied in his own mind" about his interpretation of the *Ta-hsueh* in the *Chang-chü* as the *Nien-p'u* statement cited above might suggest. [32]

In fact, even years after he wrote the preface, Chu's interest in the *Ta-hsueh* never ceased, and doubts about his own understanding of the text never completely disappeared. In a remark made sometime after his sixty-fifth year:

> When I read through my explanation of the *Chung-yung*, I have no serious doubts. But when I read the *Ta-hsueh*, I do have doubts; I am not very satisfied with it and therefore continue to revise it. [33]

And, even on those few occasions when he does show some degree of satisfaction with his understanding of the text, he is quick to admit that, with reconsideration and the passing of time, satisfaction may easily turn to dissatisfaction. In a letter to P'an Tuan-shu [34], he writes:

> This year I have revised various texts of mine once through; the revisions in the *Ta-hsueh* have been particularly numerous. Compared to my earlier work on the *Ta-hsueh*, the revised work is extremely detailed and comprehensive, yet I do not know how I will view it in the future. [35]

Such comments reveal Chu Hsi's commitment to further inquiry on the text and his lack of inhibition about revising opinions held earlier. In fact, in a letter to his most prominent disciple, Huang Kan (1152–1221), [36] sometime after the prefacing in 1189, Chu argues that only a sage or an idiot is unwilling to revise:

> I myself believed that the *Ta-hsueh* I had previously written was the final edition. But, having recently discussed it with several people, I feel that the section on "having the proper measure in one's own mind to measure

the minds of others"[37] still contains unrefined passages. The writing basically is extremely difficult to understand—one who arrives at an interpretation and sticks to it for one's whole life, if not a sage, is an idiot.[38]

It is apparent then that, even after writing the preface for the *Ta-hsueh chang-chü* in 1189, which would seem to signal the completion of his work on the text, Chu Hsi never left the *Ta-hsueh* for long. In a comment made near the end of his life at age sixty-nine, Chu speaks poignantly of his untiring devotion to the brief work:[39]

> I have expended tremendous effort on the *Ta-hsueh*. [Ssu-ma] Wen-kung wrote the [*Tzu-chih*] *t'ung-chien* (Comprehensive mirror for aid in government) and said that the strength and spirit of his whole life were exhausted on that work. The same may be said of my work on the *Ta-hsueh;* I did not expend the same strength on the *Lun-yü*, the *Meng-tzu*, or the *Chung-yung.*[40]

The profound significance he attached to the *Ta-hsueh* text is obvious.

The effort that Chu devoted to the text did not go unappreciated. Indeed his reputation for his work on the *Ta-hsueh* was such that, in 1194, when Kuang-tsung abdicated and Ning-tsung became Emperor, Chu received an imperial decree requesting that he present a lecture on the *Ta-hsueh* to the new ruler.[41]

What was the nature of Chu Hsi's scholarship on the *Ta-hsueh* during this period of nearly forty years? Three areas of particular interest to him may be singled out: 1) revision and correction of the text as it had been transmitted in its chapter form in the *Li chi;* 2) ascription of authorship, and through such ascription consolidation of the Confucian *tao-t'ung* (orthodox transmission of the Way); and 3) a systematic explanation, philological and philosophical, of the revised text. A brief description of his work in each of these areas follows.

In revising the "*Ta-hsueh*" chapter in the *Li chi*, Chu Hsi was by no means setting a precedent. As mentioned earlier, each of the Ch'eng brothers had edited it, believing that, prior to the compilation of the *Li chi*, the proper order of the "Ta-hsueh" bamboo slips had been lost and consequently the version in the *Li chi* did not accurately represent the views of the Sage.[42] Chu concurred in this opinion but still was not completely satisfied with either of the Ch'engs' editions. In his preface to the *Ta-hsueh chang-chü*, he puts it quite tactfully:

> Heaven moves in cycles: nothing goes that does not come back to its origins. So the virtuous force of the Sung appeared in all its glory, and instruction flourished. At this time, the two Ch'eng brothers of Honan appeared, and found it within their capacity to take up again the tradition of Mencius. Indeed, they were the first to give due honor to the *Greater Learning* [*Ta-hsueh*] and to make it known to the world; and, after putting the text in order, they explicated its essential points. Only then was the system of teaching employed in the school for greater learning in antiquity—the subject of the Sage's classic and worthies' commentary—brilliantly illuminated for the world again. Though I acknowledge my ignorance, I was still fortunate to have learned indirectly [from the Ch'eng brothers through their disciples and writings], so share in having heard [the tradition].

> Still, the text of the *Greater Learning* [*Ta-hsueh*] contained some errata and lacunae and hence, forgetting my rusticity, I edited it. At times, also, I took the liberty of appending my own ideas and filling in the lacunae— these await [the criticism] of superior men of the future. I know full well that I have overstepped my bounds and that there is no way for me to escape blame.[43]

And, in the first lines of his postscript to the *Chang-chü*, he again politely explains his boldness in revising the text:

> The preceding, the *Greater Learning* [*Ta-hsueh*], with a Classic portion of two hundred and five characters and a commentary of ten chapters, may presently be found in Tai [Sheng's] book on rites; but the text there is in disarray and the commentary has to some degree lost its proper order. Master Ch'eng-tzu corrected the *Greater Learning* [*Ta-hsueh*]; without considering my ability, I have ventured to rearrange the text, following his views.[44]

Chu Hsi felt that the Ch'eng brothers had been justified in making changes in the *Ta-hsueh* text but believed that their editions were still somewhat inadequate. He thus felt compelled to come out with a new edition, one which, it should be mentioned, in most respects accords with the version of the younger Ch'eng brother, I.[45] It is, of course, this edition of Chu Hsi's that, since the early Yuan era, has been considered the authorized and standard text of the *Ta-hsueh*.[46]

Chu's modifications of the traditional "Ta-hsueh" chapter as Tai Sheng transmitted it may be briefly summarized. First, he divided the text into a Classic (*ching*) portion of 205 characters and commentary (*chuan*) portion of 10 chapters. He writes:

This, the Classic portion in one chapter, may be taken as the words of Confucius, transmitted by Tseng Tzu. The ten chapters of commentary contain the ideas of Tseng Tzu, recorded by his disciples.[47]

This division into two separate portions, a Classic and a commentary, was something entirely new with Chu Hsi; neither Ch'eng I nor Ch'eng Hao had previously suggested such an arrangement (nor, for that matter, had they even divided the text into paragraphs). Chu's position here is intimately linked, of course, with his innovative view of the authorship of the text, a matter we shall take up very soon.

Second, Chu Hsi rearranged the order of the text, following many of Ch'eng I's earlier changes. According to him, there is a natural structure to the work: the Classic portion outlines the three principia (*kang-ling*) of the *Ta-hsueh*—keeping the inborn luminous Virtue unobscured, renewing the people, and coming to rest in perfect goodness[48]—together with the eight particular steps (*t'iao-mu*) by which the principia are brought to fruition—apprehending the principle in things, extending knowledge, making the thoughts true, setting the mind in the right, cultivating the person, establishing harmony in the household, governing the state well, and bringing tranquility to the empire;[49] ten chapters of commentary then elaborate, with the aid of proverbs, historical allusions, and illustrations from the Classics, these "principia" and "eight steps." In his postscript he writes:

Now, the first chapter of commentary elucidates "keeping the inborn luminous Virtue unobscured," the second chapter "renewing the people," the third chapter "coming to rest in perfect goodness" (all of the above chapters accord with Ch'eng's edition but I have added [to them the portion] from "In the *Book of Poetry* [*Shih ching*] it is said, 'Look to the coves in the banks of the Ch'i'" on down), the fourth chapter "the roots and the branches," the fifth chapter "the extension of knowledge" (both of these chapters are present arrangements), the sixth chapter "making the thoughts true" (this accords with the Ch'eng's edition), the seventh chapter "setting the mind in the right" and "cultivation of the person," the eighth chapter "cultivation of the person" and "establishing harmony in the household," and the ninth chapter "establishing harmony in the household," "governing the state well," and "bringing tranquility to the empire." There is a natural order to the work, and the ideas are all interrelated; it would seem that I have reconstructed the original form of the text. I have respectfully recorded it above in its proper order. [50]

It goes without saying that a significant rearrangement of any text will influence the way in which that text is understood. A reading of Chu Hsi's redaction of the *Ta-hsueh* indeed produces a very different understanding from that produced by a reading of the *Li chi* version of the text. [51] Whether the results of Chu's efforts to reorganize the Classic in the above "systematic" manner are valid or not is an issue still hotly debated today. Valid or not, however, his version was given the stamp of orthodoxy during the Yuan period and it maintained its exalted status until the abolition of the examination system in 1905. Thus, to appreciate the tradition's understanding of the *Ta-hsueh* text from the late Sung–early Yuan to the fall of imperial China, we must deal with Chu's version as it appears in the collection of Four Books, not the traditional version in the *Li chi*.

Chu's firm belief that Tseng Tzu had written the 10 chapters as commentary on the Classic raised a major problem for him, however. That is, whereas for all of the other "principia" and "particular steps" there existed obvious commentary portions, he could not find a corresponding commentary portion for the two steps "apprehending the principle in things" and "extending knowledge to the utmost." Chapter 4 of Tseng Tzu's commentary, according to Chu's arrangement, elucidates "the roots and the branches"; it ends with the line "This is called 'knowing the root.'" Chapter 5 of the commentary, which Chu Hsi felt should be the elucidation of "apprehending the principle in things" and "extending knowledge to the utmost" reads: "This is called 'knowing the root.' This is called 'the completion of knowledge.'" Chu is not pleased with the repetition here of the phrase "This is called 'knowing the root'" and in his commentary writes: "Master Ch'eng said, 'This is superfluous text.'" In effect, then, following Ch'eng I, he excises the phrase from the *Ta-hsueh*. That leaves him with a mere 6-character passage for Tseng Tzu's fifth chapter of commentary: "This is called 'the completion of knowledge.'" In Chu's opinion, this line alone is not sufficient explanation of the two steps *ko wu* and *chih chih*, and in his commentary on the line he asserts: "Above this line there is a hiatus in the text; this is merely the concluding phrase." Indeed *ko wu* and *chih chih* are too important to Chu Hsi to leave unexplained; hence, he takes it upon himself to "append his own ideas and fill in the lacunae"[52] in Tseng Tzu's commentary here.[53] This, then, is the third way in which Chu Hsi significantly revises the traditional "Ta-hsueh" chapter transmitted by Tai Sheng. After Tseng Tzu's line "This is called 'the completion of knowledge,'" Chu adds:

> It would appear that the preceding, the fifth chapter of commentary [by Tseng Tzu], elucidated the meaning of "fully apprehending the principle in things" and "the extension of knowledge," but it is now lost. Recently, I made bold to use the ideas of Ch'eng-tzu to supplement it as follows. . . .[54]

What has become known as the supplementary chapter of commentary (*pu-chuan*), comprising 134 characters, follows.[55] From the moment Chu Hsi's *Ta-hsueh chang-chü* began to circulate until the present day, serious questions have been raised by numerous scholars about the validity of Chu's reorganization of the *Ta-hsueh* text and, in particular, about the necessity of adding this 134-character chapter. Many a scholar since the Sung has revised the text differently;[56] however, none of their versions has ever threatened the esteemed position held by Chu Hsi's *Ta-hsueh chang-chü* in the Great Tradition.

Chu Hsi's second significant contribution to scholarship on the *Ta-hsueh* is his theory of authorship. Prior to the Sung, authorship had been ascribed to a number of chapters in the *Li chi*,[57] but not to the "Ta-hsueh." The Ch'eng brothers were the first to express opinions about the origins of the text: the elder brother, Ch'eng Hao, had called it "a work handed down from Confucius" (*K'ung-shih i-shu*); and Ch'eng I had once claimed that it was "a perfect work of the Sage" (*Sheng-jen chih wan-shu*).[58] There has been a great deal of scholarly discussion about the precise meaning of these statements, particularly Ch'eng Hao's, since it is quoted by Chu Hsi at the very outset of the *Ta-hsueh chang-chü* and is the starting point for his theories concerning the authorship of the text.[59] Some scholars interpret Ch'eng Hao's 4-character phrase "a work handed down from Confucius" to mean that Confucius simply had a hand in the *Ta-hsueh*'s editing and transmission but by no means wrote it himself. Chai Hao (1736–1788) of the Ch'ing dynasty offered the following opinion:

> I would submit that the name of the author of the *Ta-hsueh* had been lost for a long time when Ch'eng-tzu decided that it was "a work handed down from Confucius"; by mentioning Confucius he was not necessarily implying that Confucius himself wrote it. For example, the Six Classics were all edited and revised by Confucius, then transmitted to his disciples—and these are all "works handed down from Confucius." The remark [by Ch'eng-tzu] is most fitting and sound.[60]

Many contemporary scholars agree with Chai Hao's verdict that Ch'eng Hao did not mean to suggest that Confucius was the author of the *Ta-hsueh,* but rather an editor or transmitter of the text.[61] There are those who disagree, however. Chao Tse-hou, for one, argues that to state that a book has been handed down from a certain person is to regard that book as having been written by that person.[62] Regardless of what exactly the Ch'eng brothers did mean by such statements as "a work handed down from Confucius" and "a perfect work of the Sage," they were the first to link Confucius directly to the text of the *Ta-hsueh.* Their remarks indicate a firm belief that Confucius was to some degree involved in editing, revising, or writing the text and in transmitting it to later ages.

Chu Hsi's view of authorship developed out of the Ch'eng brothers' suggestion that Confucius was directly involved, in one form or another, with the *Ta-hsueh* text. In the sealed memorial of 1162 Chu claims:

> It would seem that "apprehending the principle in things" and "extension of knowledge" is what Yao and Shun called "be discriminating and undivided," and that "setting the mind in the right" and "making the

thoughts true" is what Yao and Shun called "holding fast the Mean." From antiquity on, what was transmitted by the sages and what was manifested in their conduct was nothing more than these things. As for Confucius, he gathered together all that was good but, in advancing, did not acquire the right position and thus did not practice it [i.e., all that was good] in the empire. Therefore, he withdrew and wrote it down in the form of the Six Classics in order to make it known to those of later generations who would rule the empire, the state, and the household. In these [works] he discussed the order of the root and the branches, the beginning and the end, the first and the last. The portion that is particularly detailed and clear may now be found in the book of Tai [Sheng], in the so-called 'Ta-hsueh' chapter. [63]

Confucius is credited here with putting into writing ideas transmitted through the tradition by the great sages. The ideas, to be sure, were not those of Confucius; but the words used to express those ideas were. The relationship between Confucius and the *Ta-hsueh* text is made more explicit in this memorial than it had been in the writings of Chu's predecessors. In the memorial of 1163 presented to the Emperor in Hangchou, Chu again states his view of the origin of the text:

[As for] . . . the so-called "way of greater learning," although the great sages of antiquity were born knowing it, there is not a case of one who did not [continue to] study it. Yao and Shun handed it down—such is the so-called "be discriminating, be undivided, that you may sincerely hold fast the Mean." From that time on, sage passed it on to sage, and each thereby got possession of the empire. When Confucius did not acquire the right position, he committed it to writing in order to make it known to those of later generations who would govern the empire, the state, and the household. Moreover, his disciples together transmitted it and elucidated it further. [64]

There is one important detail found here that is absent from the previous memorial: "Moreover, his disciples together transmitted it and elucidated it further." Hence, by 1163, Chu's theory of authorship was already fairly well developed: Confucius had committed to writing the "way of greater learning" as passed down by the sages of antiquity; his disciples had then transmitted the work, adding explanations of their own. Accordingly,

Chu would contend, the text of the *Ta-hsueh* should be divided into two portions, the Classic of the Sage and the commentary of the disciples.

Throughout his life, Chu Hsi associated Confucius with the authorship of the Classic chapter, but he never decisively determined Confucius's role in the actual writing. At different times, Chu suggests that Confucius had written down ideas transmitted by the ancient sages, that he had given lectures on the ancients' "way of greater learning" which disciples recorded, and finally that he had simply recited from memory the words of an ancient Classic to his disciples who then recorded it.[65] Despite such slight variations, Chu Hsi was persistent in his belief that Confucius, just by choosing to transmit or perpetuate the "way of greater learning," was in effect responsible for the composition of the chapter.

It is in the *Ta-hsueh chang-chü* and its preface that we find a significant addition to Chu Hsi's theory of authorship. Here, for the first time, Chu specifically remarks that Tseng Tzu is the disciple responsible for transmitting and explicating the text as Confucius had intended. Tseng Tzu's disciples, in turn, recorded the ideas of their master as the commentary to the Classic portion of the *Ta-hsueh*. While Chu Hsi did at times vary slightly his views of the authorship of the Classic portion of the text, he steadfastly maintained until the day he died that the commentary was the work of Tseng Tzu and his disciples. The preface of the *Chang-chü* reads:

As the Chou declined, worthy and sage sovereigns did not arise, administration of schools was not kept up, education deteriorated, mores degenerated. Though a Sage like Confucius appeared in such times, he did not attain the position of sovereign-instructor, the position from which he could enact his politics and teachings. Alone, he took the ways of the former kings, recited and passed them on to his disciples, to proclaim them to later generations.

. . . . This chapter [the "Ta-hsueh"] prominently sets forth the brilliant system of greater learning for those who have already completed the program of lesser learning: it develops the design of greater learning in all its magnitude and at the same time explores fully the details of the program of instruction.

We may presume that every one of the three thousand disciples heard this doctrine, yet only the tradition from the school of Tseng Tzu had the full authority of it. The school thus wrote a commentary to bring out its meaning. [66]

And in the body of the *Chang-chü,* immediately following the Classic portion in one chapter, Chu is briefer, but even more to the point:

This, the Classic portion in one chapter, may be taken as the words of Confucius, transmitted by Tseng Tsu. The ten chapters of commentary contain the ideas of Tseng Tzu, recorded by his disciples. [67]

Chu Hsi's disciples, it appears, are not completely satisfied with their teacher's verdict here concerning authorship. In the *Ta-hsueh huo-wen,* completed soon after the *Chang-chü,* [68] Chu is questioned:

"You, Master, have said that 'the Classic proper may be taken as the words of the Sage, transmitted by Tseng Tzu. The chapters of commentary contain the ideas of Tseng Tzu, recorded by his disciples.' How do you know this to be so?"

He answered: "The phrasing of the Classic proper is succinct, but the principles are all there. The words are easy to understand, but the import is far-reaching. Only the Sage could have done it. Yet, there is no corroborative evidence; moreover, I am inclined to think that it perhaps derived from the words of former people of antiquity. Hence, I still have doubts [about the attribution to Confucius] and dare not put it too definitively. In regard to the commentary, it quotes the words of Tseng Tzu in one instance and it also frequently accords with the *Chung-yung* and the *Meng-tzu,* so we need not doubt that it was completed by Tseng Tzu's disciples, and that Tzu-ssu handed it down to Mencius." [69]

This is the only sustained defense of his theory of authorship in all his writings. "The phrasing of the Classic proper is succinct, but the principles are all there. The words are easy to understand, but the import is far-reaching. Only the Sage could have done it." Chu Hsi is quite aware, however, that such evidence is hardly conclusive proof that the Sage himself wrote the Classic chapter. In fact, because he has no "corroborative evidence" and, moreover, is "inclined to think that it [the Classic proper] perhaps derived from the words of former people of antiquity," Chu dares not attribute authorship "too definitively" to Confucius. Instead, he states the case rather tentatively: "The Classic proper *may* be taken as the words of the Sage, transmitted by Tseng Tzu" (emphasis mine).

Concerning the commentary, however, Chu Hsi has not the slightest doubt. That the words "Tseng Tzu said" appear there, and that no other disciple is ever mentioned or quoted is evidence enough to convince Chu that "the ten chapters of commentary contain the ideas of Tseng Tzu, recorded by his disciples." Chu assumes that, since Tseng Tzu is quoted in one chapter of the commentary, the whole commentary then is likely a record of his ideas, written down by his disciples. This is a highly questionable assumption, as pointed out by a number of later scholars. [70]

In summary, Chu Hsi himself admits that Confucius's relationship to the Classic chapter is somewhat problematical; but, as noted above, never does he waver in his commitment to the position that Tseng Tzu and his disciples were directly responsible for writing and transmitting the ten chapters of commentary. [71] In a letter to Lin Tse-chih [72] Chu, referring to the *Huo-wen* passage just cited, comments:

> As for my thoughts on the Classic proper, they are mere speculation. In the commentary, the words "Tseng Tzu said" are cited, so we know that Tseng Tzu's disciples completed it. [73]

We too may indulge in a bit of speculation here. Why did Chu Hsi hold that Confucius and Tseng Tzu wrote the *Ta-hsueh* when there seemed to have been no concrete historical evidence for such a view? As has been shown, the text clearly captivated his attention; in it he found a brief but eloquent summary of Confucian ideals—personal self-cultivation and the ordering of society. Indeed, because in his mind it systematically outlined the goals of his Neo-Confucian vision, he attached tremendous importance to it. Over and over again he states that it was the most important of books, the one to be read first—even before the *Lun-yü*, the *Meng-tzu*, and the *Chung-yung*. [74] It so captured the essence of Confucianism that it must have been written by great Confucians. And that the Ch'eng brothers, his spiritual masters, had already linked it to Confucius, made a relatively explicit attribution to the Sage a simple step. Furthermore, because Tseng Tzu is quoted in the *Ta-hsueh,* Chu is able to feel confident that what he understood as a commentary to the Classic was written by Tseng Tzu and his direct disciples. For Chu the attribution to Confucius and Tseng Tzu reinforced the importance of the text: with Confucius and Tseng Tzu as the authors who could ignore the work?

A result of assigning authorship as he does was to bring about a more intimate connection among the Four Books; and this connection, in turn, increased their importance. Traditionally, Confucius had been responsible for the *Lun-yü,* Tzu-ssu for the *Chung-yung,* and Mencius for the *Meng-tzu.* By linking the *Ta-hsueh* to Confucius and Tseng Tzu, Chu Hsi was able to suggest a clear line of transmission of the *Tao (tao-t'ung)* from Confucius to Tseng Tzu, from Tseng Tzu to his disciple Tzu-ssu, and from Tzu-ssu through his disciple to Mencius. [75] The Four Books could thus almost be thought of as a unit containing the core principles of Confucianism, as passed on from Confucius to Tseng Tzu to Tzu-ssu to Mencius. According to Chu, the Ch'eng brothers, through their industrious efforts on the Four Books, had revived the orthodox transmission of the *Tao,* which had ceased with the death of Mencius. [76] (And, by implication, Chu through his own work on the texts and his relationship to the Ch'engs had continued the transmission.) The Four Books thus became the basic curriculum in a Neo-Confucian education; a profound understanding of these texts put one in direct touch with the great early Confucian thinkers and the cardinal Confucian virtues that they had transmitted.

Now we may turn to the third and final area of particular interest to Chu Hsi during his years of labor on the *Ta-hsueh*: a systematic explanation of his revised version of the text. After dividing the work into a Classic chapter and a commentary in ten chapters, rearranging the order of the *Li chi* version of the *Ta-hsueh* so that what he took to be the commentary portion would elucidate chapter by chapter the "principia" and "eight steps" outlined in the Classic portion, and adding a supplementary chapter on *ko wu* and *chih chih* to "fill in the lacunae," all of which in themselves were part of an effort to systematize the *Ta-hsueh,* Chu Hsi then wrote a line-by-line commentary on the text which was far longer and more detailed than the text itself. The revised *Ta-hsueh* text together with this commentary constitute Chu Hsi's *Ta-hsueh chang-chü.*

The commentary is more philosophical in nature than philological. However, those who attempt to discredit Chu Hsi completely by claiming that he is philologically irresponsible or unconcerned bring some discredit rather upon themselves. Almost each line of commentary begins with a number of brief philological glosses on obscure or troublesome terms in the text; a comparison of these glosses with the earlier "philological" glosses of Cheng Hsuan and K'ung Ying-ta reveals the degree to which Chu draws on those earlier commentators. And, from comments in the *Yü-lei* chapters devoted to the *Ta-hsueh* and in the *Ta-hsueh huo-wen*, we at times may see how carefully Chu Hsi considers previous glosses on the text by Cheng, K'ung, and the Ch'eng brothers before assimilating them into his commentary or rejecting them for his own glosses. I would not wish to argue that Chu's concerns in the *Chang-chü* were primarily philological or that he was always correct in his glosses, but scholars since the seventeenth century, Chinese and Westerners alike, who suggest that Chu Hsi philosophized on the Classics without the slightest regard for philological accuracy have presented a one-sided picture which is in need of correction.

The *Chang-chü* commentary attempts to show that there is a unity of structure and thought in the *Ta-hsueh*. Every effort is made by Chu to explain how one statement of the text relates to another, or one chapter to another. [77] Chu Hsi, of course, takes it on faith that a coherent message is contained in the text, for, after all, the text was composed by the sages and the worthies of the past; [78] but it must be explicated if readers are to grasp it. So, while he does not disregard philological matters, his approach to the *Ta-hsueh* may be described as principally hermeneutical.

In addition to the *Ta-hsueh chang-chü*, Chu Hsi wrote the *Ta-hsueh huo-wen* in two *chüan*, which was completed in 1189 or soon thereafter and fortunately is still extant. In fact, Chu appended a *Huo-wen* to each of his commentaries on the Four Books; but, according to the *Ssu-k'u ch'üan-shu* editors, he spent more time on the *Huo-wen* to the *Ta-hsueh* than on any of the other three. [79] The work is in a question-and-answer format that follows the order of the revised *Ta-hsueh* text. The master fields inquiries, mostly from disciples (though one cannot be certain since the questioners are not identified), regarding earlier interpretations of *Ta-hsueh* passages as well as the reasons for his own interpretations as presented in the *Chang-chü;* his responses tend to be rather lengthy philosophical expositions. Indeed, the *Huo-wen* is at least as important for understanding Chu's general philosophical outlook as it is for understanding his interpretation of the *Ta-hsueh* text.

And, in the *Chu-tzu yü-lei,* a record of conversations that took place during the period from 1170 to 1200 between Chu Hsi and his disciples, [80] five chapters (14–18) are devoted exclusively to the *Ta-hsueh.* These *Yü-lei* chapters are still another indication that, for at least thirty years from 1170 to 1200, Chu was deeply involved in a systematic inquiry into the brief text. At times the disciples raise broad interpretive questions about the meaning of passages in the *Ta-hsueh* or about comments on the text by Chu in his *Chang-chü;* but just as often they ask quite narrow philological questions concerning terms or phrases in the *Ta-hsueh* or glosses already made by Chu in the *Chang-chü* commentary.

The *Yü-lei*'s value in understanding Chu Hsi's reading and interpretation of the *Ta-hsueh* cannot be overstated; still, everything considered, the *Ta-hsueh chang-chü* is the work to be read first. If Chu's interpretation of the *Ta-hsueh* is not completely clear from a reading of the commentary, one then should proceed to the *Yü-lei* chapters; a thorough reading of the *Yü-lei* will help resolve many of the unclear points in the commentary. The *Huo-wen* too should be consulted, but it is somewhat less helpful than the *Chang-chü* and the *Yü-lei* for understanding Chu's interpretation of the *Ta-hsueh* text. In Chapter 14 of the *Yü-lei,* Chu Hsi himself remarks that the reader should concentrate first on the Classic itself and then on the *Chang-chü,* and pay little or no attention to the *Ta-hsueh huo-wen,* which in his words is but "footnotes to footnotes"[81] on the Classic.[82]

CHAPTER 4

Chu Hsi's Reading
of the *Ta-hsueh*

Chu Hsi was not the first thinker of the Sung to focus on the question of how man becomes moral. This question had preoccupied all those thinkers of the Northern Sung who would come to be regarded as the founders of Tao-hsueh, the "School of the True Way," known commonly in the West as Neo-Confucianism. Chu considered these men—Chou Tun-i, Chang Tsai, and the Ch'eng brothers—to be his spiritual masters and drew heavily on ideas advanced by them in formulating his philosophical system.[1] The Tao-hsueh or Neo-Confucian school represented a shift in emphasis in Confucian thought. Previously, attention had been given more to the problem of how to bring order and harmony to the state and the society. But, convinced that rectifying the society was a hopeless task unless those doing the rectifying had fully rectified themselves first, the Neo-Confucians were far more interested in the problem of the moral transformation of the individual. Only moral men could possibly order the society in accordance with Confucian standards.

This inward turn toward moral cultivation had its classical justification in the *Lun-yü*, where Confucius said of the *chün-tzu*, the superior man: "He cultivates himself and thereby achieves reverence." Pressed by his disciple Tzu-lu for a fuller characterization of the superior man, the Master went on to say: "He cultivates himself and thereby brings peace and security to the people."[2] From the time of Confucius on, self-cultivation and ordering the society constituted the essential aims of Confucian doctrine, "two parts of an indivisible whole."[3] But, naturally, over the centuries, different schools and thinkers would place different stress on each of these aims. Indeed, disagreement over the relative importance of the two aims frequently resulted in bitter hostility among those who associated themselves with the Confucian school.

Of course, among Sung Neo-Confucians there was little disagreement about which aim should be given more weight; the Neo-Confucians of the Northern Sung as well as Chu Hsi showed greater concern for the moral transformation of the individual. What did distinguish Chu from his predecessors, however, was the attention he gave to working out a detailed process of self-cultivation. This perhaps was Chu Hsi's greatest contribution to the Neo-Confucian school: the development of a method—a highly systematic method—of self-cultivation. So compelling was this method that it was not until some three centuries later, during the Ming dynasty, that it was forcefully challenged. From then on, Chu's thoughts on self-cultivation would be at the center of lively philosophical debate. Fiercely attacked by the so-called "subjectivists" of the Wang Yang-ming school and the *k'ao-cheng* empiricists of the Ch'ing, Chu's method nonetheless survived as part of the Neo-Confucian orthodoxy through the early decades of the present century.

The program of self-cultivation designed by Chu Hsi evolved principally out of his reading of the *Ta-hsueh*. In working out their ideas about self-perfection centuries earlier, Han Yü and Li Ao had also turned to the brief text for inspiration. They were the first Confucians to find philosophical significance in what was then an obscure chapter in the *Li chi,* initiating the long process by which the *Ta-hsueh* became one of the central texts in the Confucian tradition.[4] Chu was attracted to the *Ta-hsueh* for the same general reason that Han Yü and Li Ao had been: proclaiming that, "from the Son of Heaven on down to the commoners, all without exception should regard self-cultivation as the root,"[5] the text emphasized the critical importance of the self-cultivation process for Confucians; and it did this without slighting the political ideal of Confucianism—the ordering of society. But Chu, because of his profound, Neo-Confucian commitment to the inner moral development of the individual, showed considerably greater interest in the *Ta-hsueh* than Han Yü or Li Ao had.

The relationship between Chu's reading of the *Ta-hsueh*—or any of the Confucian Classics for that matter—and the development of his philosophical system was a highly complex one, difficult to characterize. It certainly was not a simple causal relationship in which the philosophical outlook of the man led ineluctably to a particular understanding of the text, as many scholars have presumed.[6] Rather, the relationship perhaps can best be described as dialectical. It is true that Chu approached the text with a certain philosophical predisposition, which helped to determine what he might find exciting or appealing in the text; a resonance occurred between ideas already in Chu's mind and those expressed in the text. But, as this sort of approach would suggest, the text in the process became a source of philosophical inspiration as well. The ideas found in it helped further to define, refine, and elaborate Chu's philosophical position. Chu Hsi's system of thought, thus, emerged gradually out of committed reflection on the Confucian canon, reflection that was itself affected by his philosophical beliefs.

In fact, Chu's very approach to the canon was predicated on beliefs central to his Neo-Confucian philosophy. Chu assumed that man was able to reflect meaningfully on the canon in the first place because he had the capacity to perceive the truth in the canon for himself. Specifically, because each and every individual was endowed with a mind embodying principle in all its manifestations,[7] he might with proper effort "resonate" with the principle transmitted in the sacred texts; the mind with which he was born enabled him to become awakened to the truth expressed by the sages, without excessive aid from traditional commentaries and conventional interpretation. In brief, Chu's hermeneutical assumptions owed a great deal to his ontology. But, his ontology in turn derived much of its inspiration and shape from the truth manifested in the sacred texts.

To be sure, earlier scholars also believed that the sages of the past had set down the truth in the Confucian canon; the difference between Chu and those earlier scholars was in the sorts of truths they hoped to find in the texts. Whereas pre-Sung classicists had generally looked for limited, "situational truths," that is, prescriptions detailing how to behave in life's varying circumstances and how to govern the people most effectively, Chu was seeking a universal truth, one both immanent and transcendent in the cosmos. IIis search was for the Neo-Confucian *li*, the "principle" that underlay and gave organization and unity to the entire universe. In "Shu Lin-chang so-k'an ssu-tzu hou" (A postscript to the Four Masters published at Lin-chang), completed in January 1191, Chu writes:

> The sages wrote the Classics in order to teach later generations. These texts enable the reader to reflect on the ideas of the sages while reciting their words and hence to understand what is in accordance with the principle of things. Understanding the whole substance of the proper Way, he will practice the Way with all his strength, and so enter the realm of the sages and worthies. [8]

Here, the Confucian Classics were no longer primarily prescriptive. They now manifested the one truth, or, in Neo-Confucian terms, the all-embracing principle of the universe. This principle would be revealed to any reader who struggled to "hear" their message. In "Ta Ts'ao Yuan-k'o" (A reply to Ts'ao Yuan-k'o), Chu remarks: "All things in the world have principle; the essence of principle is embodied in the works of the sages and worthies. Hence, in seeking principle, we must turn to these works." [9] And in the *Yü-lei* he says: "Read the books to understand the intentions of the sages and worthies; follow the intentions of the sages and worthies to understand natural principle." [10] Because the Confucian Classics had been written by the sages—men who fully embodied principle—they naturally were an expression of principle. [11] Through committed reflection on them one could hope to apprehend the underlying principle of the universe.

Yet, in Chu's view, the truth contained in the texts was not easy to get at, for no words could ever fully express the profound intentions of the sages. Here again, a contrast might be made with pre-Sung classical scholars. They had been intent principally on glossing, phonetically and philologically, characters and phrases whose sound or meaning was in need of elucidation. Their assumption was that, once the characters and phrases had become intelligible, the text itself would be immediately clear and meaningful to them. Understanding of the words equaled an understanding of the text. But to Chu's mind, though phonetic and philological investigation was necessary, literal understanding of the words did not equal an understanding of the text. Chu instructed his followers: "There is layer upon layer [of meaning] in the words of the sages. In your reading of them, penetrate deeply. If you simply read what appears on the surface, you will misunderstand. Steep yourself in the words; only then will you grasp their meaning."[12] And, in the same vein: "When men read a text, they merely read one layer; they do not try to get at the second layer."[13] In reading a Classic, then, the individual had to do more than run his eyes over the characters, apprehending their superficial meaning. As Chu was fond of saying, the reader should not simply read the text, he should "experience" it.[14] With an "unprejudiced mind," that is, a mind free of preconceived notions of what the text was supposed to say,[15] he had to carry on a dialogue with the text, struggling to reach an understanding with it. Without the active participation of the reader, the text and its characters had little meaning; by rediscovering the truth through serious, open dialogue with the text, the reader gave meaning to the text. Repeated encounters of this sort led the reader over time to an ever-deepening appreciation of the imbedded truth.

Chu's view of the hermeneutical task helps to explain his lifelong quest for an understanding of the *Ta-hsueh*. For forty years he revised his reading of the text, willingly modifying or abandoning earlier views, as the truth imbedded in it became increasingly apparent to him. Chu felt keenly that he had to discover for himself—no matter how much time it took—the truth manifested in the work.[16] As might be expected, this sort of personal, religious approach to the *Ta-hsueh* led to an understanding of the text that was quite new, an understanding that broke with the traditional Han through T'ang readings of the text in at least three important respects. To treat those respects in which Chu's reading differed from earlier readings is to illuminate what attracted Chu to the *Ta-hsueh;* for what was new in his understanding is what was most central to his understanding.

First, the whole orientation of Chu's interpretation of the text was

fundamentally different from that of the standard pre-Sung interpretations
of Cheng Hsuan and K'ung Ying-ta found in the *Li chi chu* and the *Li chi
cheng-i*. Cheng and K'ung viewed the work primarily as a political hand-
book for the use of the ruler alone. According to them, the chapter was
entitled "Ta-hsueh" "because it recorded extensive learning which could
be used in the administration of government."[17] Chu, in rather sharp contrast, saw the *Ta-hsueh* as a guide for self-cultivation and the ordering of
society, for the use of all men, not only the ruler; he interpreted the title
to mean "learning for adults." Chu briefly proposed this gloss for the title
in his *Chang-chü* commentary and *Ta-hsueh huo-wen*, but in his lecture on
the *Ta-hsueh* to Emperor Ning-tsung in 1194, he explained the significance
of the book's title in some detail:

> *Ta-hsueh* refers to *ta-jen chih hsueh*. In the education of antiquity there
> was learning for children (*hsiao-tzu chih hsüeh*) and learning for adults.
> Learning for children consisted in the chores of cleaning and sweeping,
> in the formalities of polite conversation and good manners, and in the
> refinements of ritual, music, archery, charioteering, calligraphy, and
> mathematics. Learning for adults consisted in the Way of probing prin-
> ciple, of cultivating the person, of establishing harmony in the house-
> hold, of governing the state well, and of bringing tranquility to the
> empire. What this work treats is the learning for adults; hence it is
> named *Ta-hsueh*.[18]

Chu Hsi thus greatly enlarged the *Ta-hsueh*'s readership, for he found in
the text a Way of cultivating the self and governing others that was to be
studied by everyone, not just by political leaders. In Chu's understanding,
the *Ta-hsueh*'s message began with the premise that all men were capable
of perfecting themselves and, indeed, should strive to do so, through a
process of self-cultivation.

Second, Chu discovered in the *Ta-hsueh* a declaration of the ontological
assumption and aim behind the self-cultivation process. The opening line
of the work reads *Ta-hsueh chih tao tsai ming ming-te* and was understood
by Chu to mean "The way of greater learning lies in keeping the inborn
luminous Virtue unobscured."[19] This reading of the line differed markedly
from the pre-Sung interpretation, "The way of great learning lies in

manifesting luminous Virtue."[20] The earlier interpretation of the phrase *ming ming-te*—"to manifest luminous Virtue"—was addressed primarily to the ruler: he was to teach his subjects morality by manifesting outwardly his own virtue throughout the land; following his example, the people too would act virtuously. By contrast, Chu Hsi took *ming ming-te*—"to keep the inborn luminous Virtue unobscured"—to be a process of inner self-perfection applicable to every man, not only to the ruler. Just as he believed the term *ta-hsueh* to refer to learning for all, so too he saw *ming ming-te* as a process relevant to all.

For Chu Hsi, *ming-te* was not outwardly expressed virtue or virtuous conduct, but rather the originally virtuous mind and nature with which every man was endowed at birth, and which might become obscured by material endowment or human desires. "To keep unobscured" or to *ming* the *ming-te* was the goal of the self-cultivation process; each individual had to seek to maintain or to regain contact with his originally good mind and nature. And, by keeping his *ming-te* unobscured, he might then cause others, through his grace and good example, to renew their *ming-te*; this was what was meant by "renewing the people" (*hsin min*).[21] In his commentary on the *Ta-hsueh* passage, Chu explained *ming-te* in some detail:

> *Ming-te* is what man acquires from Heaven; it is unprejudiced, spiritual, and completely unmuddled and thereby embodies the multitudinous manifestations of principle and responds to the myriad affairs. But it may be restrained by the endowment of *ch'i*[22] or concealed by human desire, so at times it will become obscured. Never, however, does its original luminosity cease. Therefore the student should look to the light that emanates from it and seek to keep it unobscured, thereby restoring its original condition.[23]

This explanation caused considerble controversy among Chu Hsi's disciples[24] and later Confucians of the Sung and Yuan periods.[25] They were anxious to determine whether Chu identified *ming-te* with the mind or with the nature. In fact, the explanation here seems to refer to an entity that includes both the mind and nature. Terms such as "unprejudiced" and "spiritual" clearly refer to the mind. For example, in Chapter 5 of the *Yü-lei*, Chu says, "The unprejudiced and the spiritual are by nature the original essence of the mind."[26] Furthermore, it is the mind, not the nature, that embodies the multitudinous manifestations of principle according to Chu Hsi's teachings.[27] On the other hand, his discussion of human nature in Chapter 12 of the *Yü-lei* is remarkably similar in terminology and spirit to parts of his explanation of *ming-te*. This similarity leads one to believe that *ming-te* is to be identified with the nature:

> Man's nature is originally luminous, but it is like a precious pearl immersed in dirty water where its luminosity cannot be seen. Remove the dirty water and the precious pearl is luminous of itself as before. If the individual could appreciate that it is human desire that conceals [the luminosity], enlightenment would result.[28]

Also, Chu implies in the *Yü-lei* that the nature and *ming-te* are the same by identifying each with the virtues of benevolence, righteousness, propriety, and wisdom.[29]

It would appear, then, that Chu Hsi did not understand *ming-te* in terms of either mind or nature exclusively. To appreciate his understanding of the term we should remember that for him the mind embraced both the nature and the emotions, as it had earlier in Chang Tsai's (1020–1077) philosophy.[30] For Chu, the Heaven-given Virtue (*ming-te*) referred to an entity including both the original mind, that is, the mind that shared in the mind of Heaven and was thus unprejudiced, spiritual, and unobscured, and the perfectible luminous nature within the mind. From his point of view, to keep the *ming-te* unobscured was to preserve the integrity of the original mind, a process that naturally implied the realization of the luminous nature.[31]

In Chu's reading, the *Ta-hsueh* prescribed the precise means of realizing this nature: *ko wu*. This is the third respect in which Chu's understanding of the text differed from earlier interpretations. In the opening lines of the work we read:

> Those [of antiquity] who wished to cultivate themselves first set their minds in the right; wishing to set their minds in the right, they first made their thoughts true; wishing to make their thoughts true, they first extended their knowledge to the utmost (*chih ch'i-chih*).[32]

The line that immediately follows is *chih chih tsai ko wu. Ko wu*, the final two characters of the line, is a philologically ambiguous term which has been interpreted in a variety of ways since the Han. Cheng Hsuan glossed it in this way:

> *Ko* means *lai*, "to come." *Wu* is the same as *shih*, "affair."

And he explained the line:

> When one's knowledge of the good is profound, one attracts (*lai*) good things. When one's knowledge of evil is profound, one attracts evil things. In other words, things come to a man according to what he is fond of. [33]

In this explanation, *ko wu*—the sort of thing attracted—is a consequence of *chih chih*—the sort of knowledge that is extended. K'ung Ying-ta, in his *Li chi cheng-i,* concurred in Cheng's reading of the line. Chu Hsi, however, following his spiritual master, Ch'eng I, understood *ko wu* differently:

> *Ko* means *chih*, "to arrive at," "to reach." *Wu* is the same as *shih*, "affair." *Ko wu* is "to reach to the utmost the principle in affairs and things." [34]

And his explanation of the line *chih chih tsai ko wu* was quite unlike the explanations of Cheng and K'ung, because he took *ko wu* to be the means of *chih chih* rather than its consequence:

> If we wish to extend our knowledge to the utmost, we must probe thoroughly the principle in those things that we encounter. [35]

In Chu's reading of the text, then, *ko wu* became the first step, the foundation of the self-cultivation process. That is to say, only through the apprehension of the principle in things might an individual gradually perfect himself, thereby "keeping his inborn luminous Virtue unobscured." Implicit in this method of self-cultivation was the belief that all things in the universe share a common principle. [36] Thus, understanding of the principle in external things would lead ultimately to an understanding of the principle within oneself. And, since principle in man was identical to his nature, [37] understanding of that principle would lead to self-realization.

Chu's most eloquent statement on *ko wu* and *chih chih* is found in the so-called "supplementary chapter" that he inserted into the *Ta-hsueh* text. According to Chu, originally there had been a chapter in the *Ta-hsueh* elucidating these two critical terms, but it had been lost. He therefore reconstructed" the chapter in 134 characters, drawing on ideas previously suggested by Ch'eng I. He introduced the chapter:

> It would appear that the . . . fifth chapter of commentary [by Tseng Tzu] elucidated the meaning of "fully apprehending the principle in things" and "the extension of knowledge," but it is now lost. Recently, I made bold to use the ideas of Ch'eng-tzu to supplement it as follows.[38]

The chapter reads:

> What is meant by "the extension of knowledge lies in fully apprehending the principle in things" is that, if we wish to extend our knowledge to the utmost, we must probe thoroughly the principle in those things we encounter. It would seem that every man's intellect is possessed of the capacity for knowing and that everything in the world is possessed of principle. But, to the extent that principle is not yet thoroughly probed, man's knowledge is not yet fully realized. Hence, the first step of instruction in greater learning is to teach the student, whenever he encounters anything at all in the world, to build upon what is already known to him about principle and to probe still further, so that he seeks to reach the limit. After exerting himself in this way for a long time, he will one day become enlightened and thoroughly understand [principle]; then, the manifest and the hidden, the subtle and the obvious qualities of all things will all be known, and the mind, in its whole substance and vast operations, will be completely illuminated. This is called "fully apprehending the principle in things." This is called "the completion of knowledge."[39]

It must be asked why Chu Hsi, to use his own words, would "[take] the liberty . . . of filling in the lacunae"[40] in the *Ta-hsueh* text? After all, the *Ta-hsueh* was a canonical work. How could he, a mere scholar, meddle with it? Chu must have been convinced that, after years of struggling with the text, he had come to an appreciation of its profound meaning. He had grasped the truth manifested there by the ancient sages. But the truth had been difficult to understand since some of the sages' words had been lost. He dared to "fill in the lacunae" only because doing so, he thought, would help make the truth as evident as it once had been. He was not violating the text; he carefully noted what his additions were. Chu composed the supplementary chapter in his own words and those of Ch'eng I, but the truth he expressed there, he firmly believed, was that of the sages of the past.

In "supplementing" the *Ta-hsueh*, there is little question that Chu Hsi altered its message somewhat, at least as earlier Confucians had understood it. No Han or T'ang Confucian had found in the text allusion to enlightenment or to a method for achieving it. But, in Chu's reading, *ko wu*, properly practiced, would lead ultimately to an enlightened state in which "the manifest and the hidden, the subtle and obvious qualities of all things will all be known, and the mind, in its whole substance and vast operations, will be completely illuminated." Chu read the text in this way—when earlier scholars had not—because he was bringing different concerns to the text, asking different questions of it; as an intellectual of the Sung period, following in the tradition of the Ch'eng brothers, he was predisposed toward certain philosophical issues. Which is simply to suggest that Chu did not willfully force an interpretation of the *Ta-hsueh*, but rather that he approached the text, to him the receptacle of truth, keenly sensitive to what it might reveal about issues already of some interest to him.

Enlightenment was an issue of some interest to almost all intellectuals of the Sung. With the popularity of the Ch'an school of Buddhism, Buddhist and non-Buddhist thinkers alike had been introduced to the ideal of enlightenment. In Chu's view, it was this ideal above all else that had drawn so many people, including once devout Confucians, into the Buddhist fold.[41] Naturally, I do not wish to imply that Chu merely discovered in the text of the *Ta-hsueh* a Buddhistic enlightenment. To be sure, there may be a superficial resemblance between the enlightenment described in the supplementary chapter and that of the Ch'an school, for both Chu and the Ch'an Buddhists viewed enlightenment as the total understanding of the true nature of the universe. But a brief look at their different methods of achieving enlightenment points up just how different in the end their conceptions of it were. *Ko wu*, after all, was the study of principle in external things; thus, for Chu the world out there was meaningful and closely connected to man. In rather sharp contrast, the Ch'anists believed that enlightenment could not be dependent on man's perception of external phenomena. For the external world and all its things were illusory, simply a function of discriminating consciousness. Hence, study of that world would not lead one closer to the one true reality, the Buddha-nature. Self-conscious, rational study or investigation—as called for in *ko wu*—had no validity then for the Ch'anists. In fact, even book-or-sutra learning, so critical in Chu Hsi's *ko wu*, was thought to be irrelevant. Instead, it was the intuitive understanding of one's own mind, attained through meditation, that led to the realization of the Buddha-nature within oneself.

So appealing was the simplicity and directness of the Ch'an method that even disciples of the Ch'eng brothers had turned toward Ch'an as a path to enlightenment.[42] This disturbed and frightened Chu Hsi.[43] Enlightenment, he thought, was not so simple a task as Ch'an teachings suggested. It required both inner mental composure (*ching*) *and* the thorough study of external principle (*ko wu*). For Chu, a mind completely tranquil and thus able to concentrate entirely on one thing without distraction was essential to the quest for enlightenment. But essential too was the acquisition of knowledge—moral knowledge attained through probing or investigating the principle in the world out there. Chu said: "According to our Confucian teachings 'maintaining inner mental composure' (*chü ching*) is the foundation, but 'probing principle' gives that foundation its full development."[44]

Indeed, it was largely because the Buddhists denied the value of external investigation that Chu attacked them. Quoting Ch'eng Hao, he said:

> The Buddhists devote themselves only to penetration on the higher level, not to learning on the lower level. This being the case, can their penetration on the higher level be right?[45]

Unlike the Buddhists, Chu Hsi believed that a man could not depend on his own mind alone for enlightenment. A man's dense or impure *ch'i*, the psychophysical stuff of which he was constituted, at times cut him off entirely from his nature (or principle, since they were identical). To get back to that nature required more than simple introspection; it required serious external effort as well. Only by *ko wu*, that is, by apprehending through exhaustive study the multitudinous manifestations of principle might a man in time come to understand principle and thus, by extension, his own nature.

The appeal that *ko wu* and, consequently, the brief *Ta-hsueh* text had for Chu Hsi can hardly be overstated. *Ko wu*, as Chu understood it, served as a Confucian corrective to the meditation of the Buddhists, which Chu regarded as unreliably subjectivistic: like Buddhist meditation, *ko wu* led to a realization of the self, to an enlightened state; but *ko wu* was a reality-affirming process that underscored the centrality of the relationship between self and society. To achieve enlightenment, the individual had to embrace the world; he had to seek to understand its principle, its inherent pattern. And, having apprehended this pattern, he might then readily bring his self, his household, his state, and his empire into line with it, until finally the entire world around him enjoyed complete tranquility. As Chu read in the *Ta-hsueh*:

> Only after the principle in things is fully apprehended does knowledge become complete; knowledge being complete, thoughts may become true; thoughts being true, the mind may become set in the right; the mind being so set, the person becomes cultivated; the person being cultivated, harmony is established in the household; household harmony established, the state becomes well-governed; the state being well-governed, the empire becomes tranquil. [46]

In Chu Hsi's hands, the entire orientation of the *Ta-hsueh* text had changed; a sort of "democratization" of the work had taken place. A guidebook for the political elite had now become a guidebook for anyone and everyone hoping to become part of the moral elite. That anyone might follow the program proposed by the *Ta-hsueh* and thereby join the moral elite rested on the philosophical premise, laid out in the opening lines of the *Ta-hsueh* according to Chu's reading, that each and every individual is born good—with an inborn luminous Virtue—but must struggle throughout life to keep from falling away from that good. [47] *Ko wu*, apprehending the *li* or principle in things and affairs, was the means proposed by the *Ta-hsueh* of preventing the individual from veering from the path of good; it was the process guaranteeing that one would remain constantly true to principle, the ultimate ground of man's humanity. Morally perfected oneself, one would then have a morally transforming effect on others—this was what the text meant by "renewing the people." Over time, society would come to enjoy perfect harmony and tranquility. Self-cultivation and the ordering of society thus remained as indivisible as they had always been in the Confucian tradition. The moral elite and the political elite were still inseparable.

Chu Hsi, then, gave new meaning to the *Ta-hsueh*. Years of committed reflection on the text had led to a profound appreciation of it; the philosophical assumption that principle was embodied in the mind and would be drawn by a resonance to the principle embedded in the text gave Chu the self-confidence to come to an independent reading of the Classic, breaking with traditional interpretation where necessary. Giving new meaning to the text, Chu gave new meaning to the Confucian tradition. For students of Confucianism would now read the *Ta-hsueh* as Chu Hsi had understood it. That is, his new reading would be the orthodox reading until the fall of imperial China in the early years of the twentieth century.

Notes

INTRODUCTION

1. The works would be too numerous to list in full here. The reader should refer to W. T. Chan's bibliographic essays: "The Study of Chu Hsi in the West," *Journal of Asian Studies* 35.4:555–557 (August 1976); and "Wang Yang-ming: Western Studies and an Annotated Bibliography," *Philosophy East and West* 22:75–92 (1972). Among the notable volumes to have appeared most recently are: Hok-lam Chan and Wm. Theodore de Bary, eds., *Yüan Thought: Chinese Thought and Religion under the Mongols;* de Bary, *The Liberal Tradition in China;* de Bary, *Neo-Confucian Orthodoxy and the Learning of the Mind-and-Heart;* de Bary and Irene Bloom, eds., *Principle and Practicality: Essays in Neo-Confucianism and Practical Learning;* Thomas Metzger, *Escape from Predicament: Neo-Confucianism and China's Evolving Political Culture;* Hoyt C. Tillman, *Utilitarian Confucianism: Ch'en Liang's Challenge to Chu Hsi.*

2. *Hui-an hsien-sheng Chu Wen-kung wen-chi* (hereafter cited as *Wen-chi*) 59.5a.

3. *Wen-chi* 53.17a. Wang Mou-hung (1669–1741), in his *Chu-tzu nien-p'u* (hereafter *Nien-p'u*), p. 65, dates this letter as sometime after 1183. On the *Nien-p'u*, see Conrad Schirokauer, "Chu Hsi's Political Career: A Study in Ambivalence," in *Confucian Personalities*, ed. Arthur Wright and Denis Twitchett, pp. 354–355, note 8.

4. *Yuan shih* 81, 2019.

5. Chu Hsi quotes these words of Ch'eng Hao (1032–1085) in his introductory remarks to the *Ta-hsueh chang-chü;* see *Ta-hsueh chang-chü* 1a (p. 136 of this book).

6. *Chu-tzu yü-lei* 14.2a, 14.3b, and 14.2a respectively. On the *Chu-tzu yü-lei* (hereafter *Yü-lei*), see Chapter 3, p. 45.

7. *Yü-lei* 14.2b.

CHAPTER 1

1. See *Nien-p'u*, pp. 176–178.

2. *Yü-lei* 14.1a.

3. Ibid.

4. This point is developed in Daniel K. Gardner, "Principle and Pedagogy: Chu Hsi and the Four Books," *Harvard Journal of Asiatic Studies* 44.1:57–81 (June 1984).

5. *Yü-lei* 14.1a.

6. On the *Ta-hsueh huo-wen* (hereafter *Huo-wen*), see pp. 44–45 of Chapter 3.

7. *Huo-wen* 20a.

8. A memorial presented to and approved by Emperor Wu in 141 B.C. specifically requests the dismissal of those following the teachings of Shen Pu-hai, Shang Yang,

Han Fei, Su Ch'in, and Chang I, most of whom are Legalists (*Han shu* 6, 155-156; cf. Homer Dubs, *History of the Former Han Dynasty* II, 27-28). But the *Han shu's* author, Pan Ku (A.D. 32-92), suggests that, upon taking the throne, Emperor Wu dismissed all non-Confucians from office (*Han shu* 6, 212; cf. Dubs, *History of the Former Han Dynasty* II, 119-120).

It would be a mistake to assume, however, that non-Confucians no longer played a role in the politics of the day. The *Yen-t'ieh lun,* Huan K'uan's record of an imperially sponsored debate held in 81 B.C., soon after Wu-ti's death, clearly demonstrates the importance and influence of Legalist officials at the court.

9. *Han shu* VI, 159; cf. Dubs, *History of the Former Han Dynasty* II, 32.

10. For Kung-sun Hung's memorial to the Emperor, see *Shih chi* 121.8-12; tr. Burton Watson, *Records of the Grand Historian of China* II, 399-401. Cf. *Han Shu* 88, 3593-3594, where the same memorial appears and also Dubs's discussion of the memorial in "The Victory of Han Confucianism," *History of the Former Han Dynasty* II, 346-347.

11. Ssu-ma Ch'ien, in *Shih chi* 121.12, says that, from the time of Kung-sun Hung's proposal on, "the number of literary men who held positions as ministers and high officials in the government increased remarkably." Watson, *Records* II, 401.

12. The reader should be reminded that, although Confucianism did retain its orthodox status throughout the centuries, there were periods when in influence and popularity it was eclipsed by Buddhism. For summaries of Confucianism in the Han period, see, for example, Dubs, "The Victory of Han Confucianism," *History of the Former Han Dynasty* II, 341-353; Hu Shih, "The Establishment of Confucianism as a State Religion During the Han Dynasty," *Journal of the North China Branch of the Royal Asiatic Society* 60:20-41 (1929); Tjan Tjoe Som, *Po Hu T'ung: The Comprehensive Discussions in the White Tiger Hall* I, 82-89; John Shryock, *The Origin and Development of the State Cult of Confucius,* pp. 33-47; Benjamin E. Wallacker, "Han Confucianism and Confucius in Han," in *Ancient China: Studies in Early Civilization,* ed. David T. Roy and Tsuen-hsuin Tsien, pp. 215-228; and Wang Kuo-wei, "Han Wei po-shih k'ao," *Wang Kuan-t'ang hsien-sheng ch'üan-chi* I, 156-199.

13. The editors of the *Ssu-k'u ch'üan-shu tsung-mu t'i-yao* comment (p. 717) that the *Meng-tzu* was used in the civil-service examinations from the Yuan-yu period (1086-1094) on; in fact, Wang An-shih (1021-1086) had first required all *chin-shih* candidates to demonstrate a mastery of the *Meng-tzu* in 1071 (*Hsu Tzu-chih t'ung-chien ch'ang-pien* 220.1b). The *Ssu-k'u* editors point out that, although the *Meng-tzu* was esteemed as a Classic already in the Yuan-yu period, Ch'en Chen-sun's (ca. 1190-after 1249) *Chih-chai shu-lu chieh-t'i* of the mid-thirteenth century was the first bibliography formally to classify the text under *ching,* "Classics." On the *Chih-chai shu-lu chieh-t'i,* see Teng and Biggerstaff, *Annotated Bibliography of Selected Chinese Reference Works,* p. 16.

14. This sense of mission is discussed in James T.C. Liu *Ou-yang Hsiu,* p. 19, and David Nivison, "Introduction," in *Confucianism in Action,* ed. David Nivison and Arthur Wright, pp. 4-13.

15. See note 4 to "Introduction."

16. These scholars had a good classical precedent for their critical spirit in Mencius, who said in *Meng-tzu* 7B/3: "If one believed everything in the *Book of History,* it

would have been better for the *Book* not to have existed at all. In the *Wu ch'eng* chapter I accept only two or three strips" (D. C. Lau, *Mencius, p.* 194).

17. *Shih t'ung* 14.3a–6b. For a discussion of the *Shih t'ung,* see E. G. Pulleyblank, "Chinese Historical Criticism: Liu Chih-chi and Ssu-ma Kuang," in *Historians of China and Japan,* ed. W. G. Beasley and E. G. Pulleyblank, pp. 135–166.

18. Tan and Chao's general views on the *Ch'un-ch'iu* and its commentaries are recorded in Chapter 1 of the *Ch'un-ch'iu chi-chuan tsuan-li,* compiled by Lu Ch'un. E. G. Pulleyblank, "Neo-Confucianism and Neo-Legalism in T'ang Intellectual Life," in *Confucian Persuasion,* ed. Arthur Wright, pp. 88–91, summarizes the lives of Tan and Chao and their views and work on the *Ch'un-ch'iu* and its commentaries. For other useful studies of these men and their work, see note 41 to Pulleyblank's article, p. 326.

19. P'i Hsi-jui, *Ching-hsueh li-shih,* pp. 242–246, lists and describes many Sung works on the *Ch'un-ch'iu* that were influenced by Tan and Chao. See also Ma Tsung-huo, *Chung-kuo ching-hsueh shih,* pp. 120–121. The works by these three men became the best known.

20. This comment by Lu Yu appears in Wang Ying-lin, *K'un-hsueh chi-wen* 8.22a; cited in P'i Hsi-Jui, *Ching-hsueh li-shih,* p. 212, and Ch'ü Wan-li, "Sung-jen i ching te feng-ch'i", *Ta-lu tsa-chih* 29.3.23 (August 1964). Ch'ü suggests which Confucian scholars in particular Lu had in mind.

21. On Hu Yuan, Sun Fu, and Fan Chung-yen, see Wm. Theodore de Bary, "A Reappraisal of Neo-Confucianism," in *Studies in Chinese Thought,* ed. Arthur Wright, pp. 88–94; James T. C. Liu, "An Early Sung Reformer: Fan Chung-yen," in *Chinese Thought and Institutions,* ed. John K. Fairbank, pp. 108–112; and James T. C. Liu, *Reform in Sung China,* pp. 24–25.

22. *Ou-yang Wen-chung-kung chi* 77.1a; cited in P'i Hsi-jui, *Ching-hsueh li-shih,* pp. 216–217. For a discussion of Ou-yang's views of the Confucian canon, see James T. C. Liu, *Ou-yang Hsiu,* pp. 85–99.

23. Good examples of Su's critical questioning of the *Shu ching*'s historical accuracy may be found in *Shu chuan* 6.5a–6b and 17.12a–13b; cited in P'i's *Ching-hsueh li-shih,* pp. 219–220. Ch'ü, "Sung-jen i ching te feng-ch'i," pp. 23–25, and Ma, *Chung-kuo ching-hsueh shih,* pp. 124–126, provide numerous other examples of the critical approach to the canon during the Sung. For a general discussion of the critical spirit of the early Sung, see Morohashi Tetsuji, *Jugaku no mokuteki to Sō-ju no katsudō,* pp. 512–536.

24. For a discussion of Wang's *Chou li hsin-i,* see de Bary, "Reappraisal," pp. 100–102; see also Liu, *Reform in Sung China,* pp. 30–33.

25. Both of these are translated in full in W. T. Chan, *A Source Book in Chinese Philosophy,* pp. 463–480; cf. Fung Yu-lan, *A History of Chinese Philosophy,* tr. Derk Bodde, II, 435–451.

26. Selections from it may be found in Chan, *Source Book,* pp. 484–494, and in Fung, *History* II, 454–476.

27. Two chapters from the *Cheng-meng* are translated in Chan, *Source Book,* pp. 500–514; selections from it are translated in Fung, *History* II, 478–493.

28. This is according to Ch'eng I himself; see the *I-ch'uan I chuan hsu* 3a. A few lines of this interesting preface are cited in P'i, *Ching-hsueh li-shih,* p. 224.

Of the *I-chuan I chuan* Wing-tsit Chan says, "[Ch'eng I] simply used the commentary to expound his own philosophy, often unrelated and sometimes contrary to the text." ("Chu Hsi's Completion of Neo-Confucianism," in *Etudes Song: In Memoriam Etienne Balazs*, ed. Françoise Aubin, Series II, no. 1 [1973], p. 83).

29. Chu Hsi makes this comment in *Wen-chi* 82.26a.

30. Ts'ai Yung-ch'un, *The Philosophy of Ch'eng I*, pp. 49-55, and A.C. Graham, *Two Chinese Philosophers: Ch'eng Ming-tao and Ch'eng Yi-ch'uan*, p. 145, critically discuss the contents of the *Ching-shuo*.

31. Ts'ai, *The Philosophy of Ch'eng I*, pp. 29-37, and A.C. Graham, *Two Chinese Philosophers*, pp. 141-142, critically discuss the contents of the *I-shu*.

32. Chu wrote commentaries on all of the Five Classics but the *Ch'un-ch'iu*. For summaries of his work on the Five Classics, see Takeuchi Yoshio, *Chūgoku shisō shi*, pp. 249-255, and Chan, "Chu Hsi's Completion of Neo-Confucianism," pp. 83-84.

33. *Yü-lei* 84.10b; cited in Chan, "Chu Hsi's Completion of Neo-Confucianism," p. 84. See also *Wen-chi* 14.28b; cited in P'i Hsi-jui, *Ching-hsueh li-shih*, p. 254.

34. *Yü-lei* 78.8bff; cited in Chan, "Chu Hsi's Completion of Neo-Confucianism," p. 84.

35. This point is emphasized by Ch'ien Mu, *Chu-tzu hsin hsueh-an* IV, 180-181.

36. Beginning in 1163 (see *Nien-p'u*, p. 21) until his death in 1200, he was writing commentaries and interpretive studies on the Four Books. See Gardner, "Principle and Pedagogy," pp. 57-60.

37. That the political situation and the failure of Wang An-shih's reforms led to greater interest in the "inner" realm is generally acknowledged. See, for example, Thomas Metzger, *Escape from Predicament*, pp. 75-76; de Bary, "Reappraisal," p. 105; Yü Ying-shih, "Some Preliminary Observations on the Rise of Ch'ing Confucian Intellectualism," *Tsing Hua Journal of Chinese Studies*, New Series 11.1 & 2:122 (December 1975); and Ch'ien Mu, *Chung-kuo chin san-pai nien hsueh-shu shih* I, 1-5.

38. On the Ch'eng brothers and the Four Books, see Gardner, "Principle and Pedagogy," pp. 65-67.

39. Cf. Chu Hsi's postscript to the *Chin-ssu lu* (*Wen-chi* 81.6b-7a), where he expresses a strong desire to make the tradition as accessible as possible to beginners. A translation of this postscript may be found in W.T. Chan, *Reflections on Things at Hand*, pp. 1-2. The point raised here is discussed at some length in Gardner, "Principle and Pedagogy."

40. *Yü-lei* 10.6b4-5.

41. Ch'ien Mu, "Ssu-pu kai-lun," in *Chung-kuo hsueh-shu t'ung-i*, p. 11.

CHAPTER 2

1. This date for Tai Sheng is based upon the "Ju-lin chuan" section of the *Han shu* (88, 3615), where it is stated that Tai Sheng was present at the Shih-ch'ü discussions on the Classics which took place in 51 B.C. On the Shih-ch'ü discussions, see Tjan Tjoe Som, *Po Hu T'ung* I, 91-94.

2. It would be impossible to list all the writings and opinions on the authorship and date of the "Ta-hsueh" chapter. Modern scholarship that summarizes or represents the different historical and contemporary views on these matters includes: Kao Ming, "Ta-hsueh pien," in *Li-hsueh hsin-t'an*, particularly pp. 100-107; Chao

Tse-hou, *Ta-hsueh yen-chiu*, pp. 1–74, 94–95; Takeuchi Yoshio, "Daigakuhen seiritsu nendai kō" in *Rōshi genshi*, pp. 265–272; Akatsuka Kiyoshi, *Daigaku Chūyō*, pp. 25–28; Yamashita Ryūji, *Daigaku Chūyō*, pp. 15–17; Fung Yu-lan, "Ta-hsueh wei Hsun-hsueh shuo," *Yen-ching hsueh-pao* 7:1319–1326 (1930); Tai Chün-jen, "Hsun-tzu yü *Ta-hsueh Chung-yung*", *K'ung-Meng hsueh-pao* 15:91–103 (1968); Hsu Fu-kuan, *Chung-kuo jen-hsing lun shih*, pp. 266–273; and Ch'ien Mu "Ssu-pu kai-lun," p. 10.

For general discussions of the history of the *Ta-hsueh* text that have been helpful in preparing this chapter, see Akatsuka, *Daigaku Chūyō;* Yamashita, *Daigaku Chūyō;* Fumoto Yasutaka, "Daigaku o chūshin to shitaru Sōdai jugaku," *Shinagaku kenkyū*, 3:269–309 (1949); and Toda Toyosaburō, "Sōdai ni okeru Daigakuhen hyōshō no shimatsu," *Tōhōgaku* 21:46–56 (1961).

3. An account of K'ung's work on the Five Classics appears in the "Ju-hsueh chuan" section of the *Chiu T'ang shu* (189A, 4941) and is cited in Morohashi Tetsuji, *Keigaku kenkyū josetsu*, pp. 63–64. For an interesting discussion of the *Wu-ching cheng-i*, see Nagasawa Kikuya, *Shina gakujutsu bungeishi*, pp. 145–149.

4. The standard edition of the *Li chi cheng-i* with Cheng Hsuan's commentary and K'ung Ying-ta's subcommentary is found in the 1815 edition of the *Shih-san ching chu-shu*, ed. Juan Yuan (1764–1849).

5. As Wei-ming Tu suggests, "The importance of ritual studies in Confucian scholar-ship under the sponsorship of the T'ang court must have aroused a considerable inter-est in the *Book of Rites* of which the *Great Learning* and the *Doctrine of the Mean* are particularly significant as comprehensive reflections on the Confucian way of life." See Tu, "The Great Learning in Neo-Confucian Thought" (paper presented at the Annual Meeting, Association for Asian Studies, 19 March 1976, Toronto), p. 1. The popularity of ritual studies in the T'ang is mentioned in Honda Nariyuki, *Ching-hsueh shih-lun*, tr. Chiang Hsia-an, p. 276.

6. For discussions of Han Yü, see Fung Yu-lan, *History* II, 408–413 and de Bary, "Reappraisal," pp. 83–88.

7. *Chu Wen-kung chiao Ch'ang-li hsien-sheng wen-chi* 11.1a–4b; for partial transla-tions of "Yuan tao," see W. T. Chan, *Source Book*, pp. 454–456, and de Bary, ed., *Sources of Chinese Tradition* I, 376–379.

Shimada Kenji, *Shushigaku to Yōmeigaku*, pp. 17–26, discusses the significance of "Yuan tao" in T'ang and Sung intellectual history.

8. *Ch'ang li hsien-sheng wen-chi* 11.3a1–3.

9. Ibid. 11.3a3–5; Chan, *Source Book*, p. 455 (with modification here).

10. A discussion of Li Ao may be found in Fung, *History* II, 413–422. On his re-lationship with Han Yü, see p. 413. As to his dates, *Chiu T'ang shu* 160, 4209, says that he died in the middle of the Hui-ch'ang period (841–846).

11. *Li Wen-kung chi* 2.5a–13b; partial translations of "Fu-hsing shu" appear in Chan, *Source Book*, pp. 456–459, and Fung, *History* II, 413–421.

12. Toda, "Sōdai ni okeru Daigakuhen," p. 50, lists the number of items Li Ao quotes from each of the Confucian works: *Shih ching*, 1; *Li chi*, 3; *Tso chuan*, 2; *I ching*, 19; *Chung-yung*, 15; and *Lun-yü, Meng-tzu*, and *Ta-hsueh* together, 21.

13. Cf. Fung, *History* II, 414.

14. *Li Wen-kung chi* 2.8b; Fung, *History* II, 420 (with slight modification here).

15. *Li Wen-kung chi* 2.9a; Fung, *History* II, 420 (with modification here).

16. *Li Wen-kung chi* 2.9a; Fung, *History* II, 420–421 (with modification here).

17. *Li Wen-kung chi* 2.9a; Fung, *History* II, 421 (with modification here).

18. *Li Wen-kung chi* 2.9a–b.

19. Ibid. 2.9b.

20. On the *Yü-hai*, see Teng and Biggerstaff, pp. 92–93.

21. The Ch'iung-lin Gardens were imperial gardens located to the west of K'ai-feng, established in the 2nd year of the Chien-te period of the Sung dynasty (964), which became the site for banquets hosted by the emperor in honor of successful candidates in the imperial examination.

22. *Yü-hai* 34.3b; according to *Yü-hai* 34.3b–4a, the "Ta-hsueh" was conferred upon successful *chin-shih* on the following dates also: 3 June 1038, 4 June 1046, and 16 May 1061.

23. On the *Sung hui-yao chi-kao*, see Teng and Biggerstaff, pp. 117–118.

24. *Sung hui-yao chi-kao* 5696.6–7 (p. 4248). This information is also contained in the *Shih-wu chi-yuan chi-lei* (Teng and Biggerstaff, pp. 102–103) by Kao Ch'eng (fl. during Sung Yuan-feng period [1078–1085]), p. 249.

25. For a list and discussion of memorials and essays containing references to the "Ta-hsueh" by these men, see Fumoto, "Daigaku," pp. 272–275. See also Akatsuka, *Daigaku Chūyō*, p. 9.

26. See note 22 above.

27. Record of the work appears in the Sung bibliography *Chih-chai shu-lu chieh-t'i* by Ch'en Chen-sun (p. 45), and in the bibliographic section of the *Sung shih* (202.14a8–9). Chu I-tsun (1629–1709), in his *Ching-i k'ao* (Teng and Biggerstaff, pp. 41–42) 156.1a, says that he has not seen it and the *Ssu-k'u ch'üan-shu tsung-mu*, completed in 1782, has no entry at all for it. The last definite reference to it appears in the late Ming; as the *Ching-i k'ao* (156.1a) and Fumoto (p. 276) point out, Ch'en Ti's (1541–1617) bibliography *Shih-shan t'ang tsang-shu mu-lu* does contain an entry for the *Ta-hsueh kuang-i* in one *chüan* by Ssu-ma Kuang (p. 8). (The *Chung-yung kuang-i* is also recorded on p. 9.) Thus we may assume that the *Ta-hsueh kuang-i* was extant until the late Ming but was lost sometime before the *Ssu-k'u* compilation in the mid-Ch'ing.

28. *Wen-kuo Wen-cheng Ssu-ma kung wen-chi* 71.10a–11a.

29. Ibid., 71.10a.

30. Ibid., 71.11a.

31. *Li chi chu-shu* 60.1b; cf. D.C. Lau, "A Note on Ke Wu," *Bulletin of the School of Oriental and African Studies* 30:353 (1967).

32. For a brief comparison of these interpretations of the line, see Yamashita, *Daigaku Chūyō*, p. 23.

33. *Chang-tzu ch'üan-shu*, p. 110; cited in Fumoto, "Daigaku," p. 276.

34. For the location of these references in Chang's collected works, see Fumoto, "Daigaku," pp. 276–277.

35. Brief discussions of the Ch'eng brothers' contribution to the *Ta-hsueh* may be found in Akatsuka, *Daigaku Chūyō*, p. 10; Fumoto, "Daigaku," pp. 277–278; and Yamashita, *Daigaku Chūyō*, pp. 23–30.

36. "Ming-tao hsien-sheng hsing-chuang" in *I-ch'uan hsien-sheng wen-chi* 7.6b. The terms in single quotation marks here are all from the *Ta-hsueh*.

37. *Ho-nan Ch'eng-shih i-shu*, p. 18.

38. Ibid., p. 303.

39. Ibid., p. 341.

40. Ch'eng Hao's version, *Ming-tao hsien-sheng kai-cheng Ta-hsueh*, may be found in *Ho-nan Ch'eng-shih ching-shuo* 5.1a–3a. Ch'eng I's version, *I-ch'uan hsien-sheng kai-cheng Ta-hsueh*, may be found in the same work 5.3a–5b.

41. *I-shu*, p. 341. See also Chu Hsi's comment in his "Ta-hsueh chang-chü hsu" 2b, which precedes the text of the *Ta-hsueh* in the *Ssu-pu pei-yao* edition (p. 134 of this book); the translation of this passage appears on p. 85.

42. The differences between the versions of Ch'eng Hao and Ch'eng I are quite significant; in fact, Chu Hsi seems to draw almost exclusively on Ch'eng I's version. Yamashita, *Daigaku Chūyō*, pp. 23–30, and Chao Tse-hou, *Ta-hsueh yen-chiu*, pp. 76–88, compare the various versions of the *Ta-hsueh*. Chu Hsi acknowledges his indebtedness to Ch'eng I's revisions in the *Ta-hsueh chang-chü* 2b (p. 139; see the translation, p. 94) and "Chi Ta-hsueh hou" in *Wen-chi* 81.9b (p. 159; see the translation, p. 126).

43. *I-shu*, p. 214; cf. Graham, p. 17, and Chan, "The Evolution of the Neo-Confucian Concept *Li* as Principle" in *Neo-Confucianism, Etc.*, p. 73. What is in quotation marks here is from *Shih ching* #260/2 and is quoted in *Meng-tzu* 6A/6. In *I-shu*, p. 216, Ch'eng I comments: "The innumerable manifestations of principle in the end are but one principle"; cf. Graham, p. 11.

44. *Wai-shu* 2.4a; Graham, p. 74 (with modification here).

45. *I-shu*, p. 209; Chan, *Source Book*, p. 561 (with modification here). Cf. Graham, p. 76 and Fung, *History*, II, 529.

46. See Graham's discussion of this point, pp. 79–80.

47. What is in quotation marks here is from *Ta-hsueh*, "Classic," par. 4.

48. From *Shang shu* 5.14b; cf. James Legge, *The Chinese Classics* III, 87.

49. *I-shu*, p. 209; cf. Chan, *Source Book*, pp. 560–561, and Graham, p. 76.

CHAPTER 3

1. Throughout this book, ages are given in Chinese *sui*; the Western equivalent may be obtained by subtracting one.

2. On the *Chu-tzu nien-p'u*, see note 3 of the "Introduction."

3. *Nien-p'u*, p. 168. For each of the Four Books, Chu wrote a *Huo-wen*. Together they are known as the *Ssu-shu huo-wen*; on the *Huo-wen*, see pp. 44–45.

4. Actually, there is evidence indicating that Chu was familiar with the text much earlier. According to the *Nien-p'u* (p. 3), Chu was first instructed in the *Ta-hsueh* by his father, Chu Sung (1097–1143), in 1140 at age 11. (See Chu Sung's short biographical notice together with a listing of relevant biographical material in *Sung-jen chuan-chi tzu-liao so-yin*, hereafter cited as *SJCC*, pp. 569–570).

And in 1156, as a subprefectural registrar in T'ung-an, Fukien, Chu Hsi wrote:

Learning begins with knowledge. Only the apprehension of the principle in things is sufficient to extend that knowledge, and, when knowledge is extended, the thoughts become true and the mind set in the right; in this way, the order [described] in the *Ta-hsueh* is carried out thoroughly and without difficulty. (*Wen-chi* 77.4b–5a)

But neither the *Nien-p'u* entry nor the *Wen-chi* comment reveals a particularly strong commitment to the text yet.

5. *Nien-p'u*, pp. 18–19. Schirokauer, p. 166, mentions this memorial.

6. *Wen-chi* 11.3a–b. The terms that appear here, *the apprehension of the principle in things, the extention of knowledge, the thoughts will become true,* and *the mind will become set in the right,* are all key phrases in the text of the *Ta-hsueh.*

7. "Be discriminating and undivided" and "holding fast the Mean" are allusions to *Shang shu* 4.8b; I follow Legge's *Chinese Classics* III, 61–62. Here Chu Hsi paraphrases the *Shang shu;* I have modified Legge's translation to accord with Chu's changes.

8. *Wen-chi* 11.3b–4a.

9. *Nien-p'u*, pp. 19–20. These three memorials of 1163 are briefly described in Schirokauer, pp. 166–167.

10. This is "Classic," par. 6 of the *Ta-hsueh.*

11. "Harmony is established in the household," "the state becomes well-governed," and "the empire becomes tranquil" are all important terms from the *Ta-hsueh.*

12. The idea expressed in the memorial up to this point is straight from *Ta-hsueh,* "Classic," pars. 4–5.

13. This is a definition of *ko wu* suggested first by Ch'eng I; see, for example, *Honan Ch'eng-shih i-shu,* pp. 347, 209.

14. A direct quotation from *Shang shu* 4.8b; Legge, *Chinese Classics* III, 61–62.

15. *Wen-chi* 13.1a–b.

16. In the *Nien-p'u,* p. 213, it is recorded that, in December 1194, Chu Hsi went to Yü-shan to give a lecture at the district school; the District Magistrate, a certain Ssu-ma Mai, then published the lecture notes to make them known to all. Po Shou-i, *Ts'ung-cheng chi chiang-hsueh chung-te Chu Hsi,* p. 37, cites this *Nien-p'u* entry.

17. This is criticism of the circumstances prevailing during Chu Hsi's lifetime.

18. "Yü-shan chiang-i" in *Wen-chi* 74.19b.

19. This letter is cited in the *Nien-p'u,* p. 169.

20. See a short biographical notice in *SJCC,* pp. 2152–2153.

21. *Wen-chi* 39.17b.

22. A biographical notice may be found in *SJCC,* pp. 1212–1215.

23. This letter is cited in the *Nien-p'u,* p. 169.

24. No work with this title survives. However, in the *Nien-p'u,* p. 169, Wang Mou-hung suggests that the *Hsiang-shuo* is a draft version of the *Huo-wen.*

25. *Wen-chi* 33.26a.

26. This letter appears in the *Nien-p'u,* p. 169.

27. See his biography in *SJCC,* pp. 2268–2271.

28. *Wen-chi* 31.16b.

29. *Nien-p'u,* p. 226.

30. Comments about revision of the *Ta-hsueh* appear, for example, in letters dating from 1190 and 1196 (*Wen-chi* 62.1a and 63.23a); these letters are referred to in the *Nien-p'u,* p. 66.

31. *Yü-lei* 14.9a. This comment is recorded by Chu's pupil, Ch'en Ch'un (1153–1217), whose notes, according to the *Yü-lei* preface, date from the years 1190 and 1199. Given the tone of the question, I would say that this comment was made rather soon after the completion of the *Chang-chü* in 1189. Ch'ien Mu in his *Chu-tzu hsin hsueh-an* IV, 214–215, also dates it 1190 rather than 1199.

32. In a letter to Ying Jen-chung (*SJCC,* p. 4092) Chu Hsi comments:

I have repeatedly revised the *Ta-hsueh* and the *Chung-yung;* still they are not perfect. And only now does the *Ta-hsueh* seem to have somewhat fewer defects. The principles [of the work] are explained best when discussed orally; when I put them on paper, I am able to get at only a very small percentage of them (*Wen-chi* 54.11a–b).

There is no way to date this letter precisely, for it is extremely brief and provides absolutely no internal evidence. Ch'ien Mu, however, on completely unconvincing grounds, argues that it must have been written sometime after Chu left his prefectural post in Chang-chou in Fukien in 1191; see *Chu-tzu hsin hsueh-an* IV, 216. Although I do not agree wtih Ch'ien's line of reasoning in the *Hsin hsueh-an*, because of the reference to repeated revisions, I too would date the letter rather imprecisely to Chu's later years.

33. *Yü-lei* 19.9b. This comment is from the record of Wang Kuo (*SJCC*, pp. 194–195); according to the *Yü-lei* preface, his record contains remarks made during the period from 1194 until Chu's death.

34. *SJCC*, p. 3636.

35. *Wen-chi* 50.4a. This letter cannot be dated precisely; the only clue we have to its date is in the *Nien-p'u*, p. 67, where Wang Mou-hung states that it was written sometime after 1183.

36. His biography may be found in *SJCC*, pp. 2865–2866.

37. *Ta-hsueh*, "Commentary," X.2.

38. *Hui-an hsien-sheng Chu wen-kung hsu-chi* 1.3b. This last line derives from *Lun-yü* 17/3; Legge, *Chinese Classics* I, 318.

39. From the notes taken in 1198 by Kuo Yu-jen.

40. *Yü-lei* 14.10a. Cf. also *Yü-lei* 14.9b–10a.

41. *Nien-p'u*, p. 202. For a brief account of Chu Hsi's 40-day lectureship at court, see Schirokauer, pp. 182–183. The complete record of this lecture on the *Ta-hsueh* is preserved in *Wen-chi* 15.1a–20b.

42. See p. 24.

43. "Ta-hsueh chang-chü hsu" 2b–3a (pp. 134–135); see the translation, pp. 85–86.

44. "Chi Ta-hsueh hou" in *Wen-chi* 81.9b (p. 159); see the translation, p. 126. For another comment about the disorder of the old version of the "Ta-hsueh," see Chu's remark in the *Ta-hsueh chang-chü* 2a–b, immediately following the Classic chapter of Confucius (pp. 138–139); it appears in the translation on p. 94.

45. See note 42 to Chapter 2.

46. See note 4 to "Introduction."

47. *Ta-hsueh chang-chü* 2a–b (pp. 138–139); see the translation, p. 94.

48. Chu Hsi calls these items the three principia in *Chang-chü* 1b.1 (p. 137); see note 55 to the translation.

49. Chu Hsi calls these things the eight particular steps in *Chang-chü* 2a.1 (p. 138); see note 64 to the translation.

50. "Chi Ta-hsueh hou" in *Wen-chi* 81.9b (p. 159); see the translation, pp. 126–127. What appears in parentheses here are interlinear notes made by Chu Hsi himself.

51. Chapter 4 discusses some of the philosophical implications of Chu's changes.

52. "Ta-hsueh chang-chü hsu" 2b–3a (pp. 134–135); see the translation, p. 86.

53. For all of the above passages and Chu Hsi's comments on them, see my translation of *Ta-hsueh*, "Commentary," IV–V.

54. *Ta-hsueh*, "Commentary" V.

55. For the supplementary chapter, see *Ta-hsueh*, "Commentary" V. The significance of this chapter is discussed in Chapter 4.

56. For a list of some of these scholars and their revisions, see: Chao Tse-hou, pp. 88–93; Ts'ai Jen-hou, "Ta-hsueh fen-chang chih yen-chiu," *K'ung-Meng hsueh pao*, 9:65–66 (1965); Kao Ming, pp. 110–120; Yamashita, pp. 32–55; and T'ang Chün-i, "Ta-hsueh chang-chü pien-cheng chi ko wu chih shih ssu-hsiang chih fa-chan," *Ch'ing-hua hsueh-pao*, New Series 4.2:12 (February 1964).

57. Kao Ming, pp. 100–101, lists these chapters and their putative authors.

58. *Ch'eng-shih i-shu*, pp. 18, 341 respectively.

59. See Chu's comment prior to the Classic chapter of the *Ta-hsueh* (p. 136); the translation appears on p. 87.

60. Chai Hao, *Ssu-shu k'ao-i* 1.2a.

61. Among these scholars is Kao Ming; see *Li-hsueh hsin-t'an*, p. 101.

62. Why then, Chao asks in his *Ta-hsueh yen-chiu*, p. 2, would Chai Hao interpret Ch'eng Hao's statement as he does? The probable answer, he speculates, is that Chai himself believed that the *Ta-hsueh* was not written by Confucius and wished to conceal Ch'eng's error; he therefore purposely misrepresented Ch'eng's view.

63. *Wen-chi* 11.3b–4a.

64. *Wen-chi* 13.1a–b.

65. Wen-chi 1518a.

66. "Ta-hsueh chang-chü hsu" 1b–2a (pp. 132–133); see the translation, pp. 82–83.

67. *Ta-hsueh chang-chü* 2a–b (pp. 138–139); see the translation, p. 94.

68. We cannot be absolutely certain about the completion date of the *Huo-wen*. According to Wang Mou-hung, Chu Hsi had written a draft of the *Ta-hsueh huo-wen* as early as 1174; see the letter to Lü Tsu-ch'ien on p. 31. Also in the *Nien-p'u* entry for 1189 (p. 168), after writing that Chu Hsi completed the prefaces for the *Ta-hsueh* and *Chung-yung chang-chü*, Wang quotes an earlier *nien-p'u* that says that, for each of these works, Chu wrote a *Huo-wen*. This would suggest that, in Wang's opinion, the final draft of the *Ta-hsueh huo-wen* was completed at the same time or soon after the prefacing of the *Ta-hsueh chang-chü*.

69. *Ta-hsueh huo-wen* 19a. For a discussion of this passage, see Chao Tse-hou, pp. 22–23.

70. Kao Ming discusses the objections raised by scholars to Chu Hsi's views in his section on the authorship of the *Ta-hsueh*, pp. 100–107. See also Chao Tse-hou's objections, pp. 17–24.

71. In his Imperial Lecture on the *Ta-hsueh* presented in 1194, he repeats nearly word for word what he had written about the commentary chapters five years earlier in the *Chang-chü*: "The commentary portion in 10 chapters contains the ideas of Tseng Tzu, recorded by his disciples" (*Wen-chi* 15.8a). But his comment about the Classic chapter differs slightly from the earlier statements in the memorials, the *Chang-chü*, and the *Huo-wen*: "The Classic portion of the *Ta-hsueh* . . . it would seem contains the words of an ancient Classic recited by the Sage and recorded by Tseng Tzu." (*Wen-chi* 15.8a) This is the first time we come across the suggestion that the *Ta-hsueh* had been a Classic committed to writing in olden times; the implication here would seem to be that, somehow or other, its transmission had ceased, only to be revived by the Sage, who recited it to his disciples.

72. A brief biographical notice appears in *SJCC*, p. 1378.

73. *Hui-an hsien-sheng Chu Wen-kung wen pieh-chi* 6.7b.

74. See, for example, *Ta-hsueh huo-wen* 19b–20b and numerous comments in Chapter 14 of the *Yü-lei*, particularly 14.1a–2b. Why Chu ordered the Four Books as he did is taken up in Gardner, "Principle and Pedagogy."

75. On the *tao-t'ung*, see Wing-tsit Chan's discussion in "Chu Hsi's Completion of Neo-Confucianism," pp. 73–81. Chu's prefaces to the Four Books discuss the transmission of the Tao in great detail.

76. See, for example, Chu Hsi's prefaces to the *Chung-yung chang-chü* and the *Ta-hsueh chang-chü*.

77. A reading of the notes to "An Annotated Translation of the *Ta-hsueh* Following Chu Hsi's Reading" will make this evident.

78. See Daniel K. Gardner, "Chu Hsi's Reading of the *Ta-hsüeh*: A Neo-Confucian's Quest for Truth," *Journal of Chinese Philosophy* 10.3:183–204 (September 1983).

79. See *Ssu-k'u ch'üan-shu tsung-mu t'i-yao*, p. 722.

80. The *Yü-lei* in 140 *chüan* was compiled in 1270 by Li Ching-te (fl. 1263) from 5 already existing collections of conversations between Chu and his disciples; these collections were based on the notes recorded by the disciples. Ichikawa Yasuji's "Shushi gorui zakki," *Jinbun kagakuka kiyō* 21:137–184 (1959), discusses the background of the *Yü-lei* and its compilation and provides a chart (based on the preface to the *Yü-lei*) for dating the conversations recorded in the text.

81. Yü-lei 14.9a.

82. See comments, for example, in *Yü-lei* 14.8a, 14.8b, 14.9a, and 14.9b. I wish to emphasize that the *Huo-wen*, though not quite so important as the *Chang-chü* or the *Yü-lei*, is nonetheless essential reading for those hoping to understand Chu Hsi's interpretation of the *Ta-hsueh*. The "footnotes to footnotes" provide philological and philosophical elaboration of Chu's reading of the *Ta-hsueh*, often when we are in most need of it. As the reader will find, my annotated translation frequently draws on the *Huo-wen*.

CHAPTER 4

1. See Chan, "Chu Hsi's Completion of Neo-Confucianism," particularly pp. 61–73.

2. *Lun-yü* 14/45; D. C. Lau, *The Analects*, p. 131.

3. Benjamin I. Schwartz, "Some Polarities in Confucian Thought," in *Confucianism in Action*, ed. David Nivison and Arthur Wright, p. 52.

4. See Chapter 2, "The *Ta-hsueh* Before Chu Hsi."

5. *Ta-hsueh*, "Classic," par. 6.

6. There has been an unfortunate temptation on the part of many scholars since the Sung, Chinese and non-Chinese alike, to view Chu Hsi's innovative understanding of the *Ta-hsueh* merely as an outgrowth of his Neo-Confucian philosophical system. Some, particularly the Ch'ing *k'ao-cheng* scholars, even have gone so far as to argue that Chu turned to the *Ta-hsueh*, and to the other texts in the Confucian canon as well, principally to justify an elaborate philosophical program that, in truth, was not situated firmly in the Confucian tradition; implicit in this point of view is the belief that the formulations of the Ch'eng-Chu school were not genuinely Confucian and that Chu's reading of the Confucian canon was artful manipulation, intended solely to provide Confucian legitimacy for a school of thought in need of it. This viewpoint completely fails to appreciate the deep reverence Chu Hsi and other thinkers

of the Ch'eng-Chu school felt toward the Confucian Classics and the inspirational role those texts played in the development of Neo-Confucian thought.

7. For example, see *Yü-lei* 5.6b.

8. *Wen-chi* 82.26a.

9. *Wen-chi* 59.5a.

10. *Yü-lei* 10.2a.

11. Cf. Ichikawa Yasuji, *Tei I-sen tetsugaku no kenkyū*, pp. 131–137.

12. *Yü-lei* 10.2a.

13. *Yü-lei* 10.2a.

14. For example, see *Yü-lei* 10.4b.

15. *Wen-chi* 55.9a. The importance of the "unprejudiced mind" is discussed in Ch'ien Mu, *Chu-tzu hsin hsueh-an* III, 613–687 passim.

16. A lengthy discussion of Chu Hsi's method of reading may be found in Daniel K. Gardner, "Transmitting the Way: Chu Hsi and His Program of Learning."

17. *Li chi chu shu* 60.1a; this is a modification of a translation found in the notes on the "Title of the Work" in Legge, *Chinese Classics* I, 355.

18. *Wen-chi* 15.1a. See note 52 to the translation of the *Ta-hsueh* for more about Chu's understanding of the title.

19. *Ta-hsueh*, "Classic," par. 1.

20. *Li chi chu-shu* 60.1a.

21. See *Ta-hsueh*, "Classic," par. 1, and Chu Hsi's commentary on it (p. 136).

22. According to Chu Hsi, *ch'i* is the stuff of which the entire universe and all things in it, including man, are composed. I would translate the term *ch'i* as "psychological stuff," because it designates not just material substance but functions and activities of the mind as well. Each thing in the universe is endowed with *ch'i*; it is the relative density and purity of its *ch'i* that gives the thing its peculiar form and individual characteristics. The relationship between *li*, "principle," and *ch'i* is clearly stated by Chu: "There has never been any *ch'i* without principle nor any principle without *ch'i*" (*Yü-lei* 1.1b; cf. Chan, *Source Book*, p. 634). The two entities cannot exist independently of each other; without principle, the *ch'i* has no ontological reason for being; and, without *ch'i*, principle has nothing to adhere to. Evil arises in man because his particular allotment of *ch'i* (the amount and quality of which varies from man to man) is dense or impure and so obscures his principle, the basis of his humanity.

23. This is from the *Chang-chü* commentary to *Ta-hsueh*, "Classic," par. 1 (p. 136).

24. See, for example, questions put to Chu Hsi in *Yü-lei* 14.11b–18a.

25. See their discussions about the nature of *ming-te* in *Ssu-shu ta-ch'üan* 1.1b–3a.

26. *Yü-lei* 5.5b. Also, in *Yü-lei* 5.3b, when asked whether the seat of the spiritual is the mind or the nature, Chu responds: "The seat of the spiritual is the mind alone; it is not the nature. Nature is simply principle." Again, in *Yü-lei* 5.6b, we read: "Although the mind is a distinct entity, it is unprejudiced and therefore able to embody the multitudinous manifestations of principle."

27. For instance, *Yü-lei* 5.6b (cited in the previous note).

28. *Yü-lei* 12.8a; Fung, *History* II, 560 (with modification). And in *Yü-lei* 4.17b we encounter a similar passage:

Once there is such-and-such a manifestation of principle there is such-and-such a *ch'i*. Once there is such-and-such a *ch'i* there is necessarily such-and-such a manifestation of principle. It's just that he who receives clear *ch'i* is a sage or worthy—he is like a precious pearl lying in crystal clear water. And he who receives turbid *ch'i* is an idiot or a degenerate—he is like a pearl lying in turbid water. What is called "keeping the inborn luminous Virtue unobscured" is the process of reaching into the turbid water and wiping clean this pearl.

In this way, the principle or the nature becomes manifestly luminous once again.

29. The Sung Neo-Confucians, in accord with the Mencian view of the original goodness of human nature, believed human nature to be comprised of these four virtues (e.g., *Yü-lei* 5.2a and 6.9a). In 14.13b, *ming-te* too is said to be comprised of these four virtues:

Men all originally embody *ming-te*. Within the *te* there exist the four virtues, benevolence, righteousness, propriety, and wisdom. It is only that they are confused by external things and thus become obscured, and so they all decay. Therefore, in the way of greater learning it is necessary first to keep the *ming-te* unobscured.

And again, in 14.12a, Chu Hsi is asked whether *ming-te* is the nature of benevolence, righteousness, propriety, and wisdom, to which he responds, "Yes, it is." See also *Yü-lei* 14.22a-b.

30. For Chang Tsai's comment, see *Chang-tzu ch'üan-shu*, p. 290.

31. The hitherto ignored importance of the mind in Chu Hsi's thought is discussed at great length in Ch'ien Mu's *Chu-tzu hsin hsueh-an* and in Wei-ming Tu's review of Ch'ien's book in *The Journal of Asian Studies*, 33.3:441–454 (May 1974). Tu, in commenting upon Chu's understanding of the mind, says (p. 446):

In his discussion of the human mind (*jen-hsin*) and ontological mind (*tao-hsin*), he signified that the human mind, conditioned by the "self-centeredness of the material being" (*hsing-ch'i chih ssu*), can be transformed through moral cultivation to become identified with the ontological mind. Such an identification enables the ontological mind, which is the true basis of humanity, to manifest the "heavenly principle" in human affairs. It is therefore important for one to cultivate the mind so that, despite the inherent limitation of the physical self, it can "embody" principle, which is the ultimate ground of human nature.

This explanation of the mind is helpful in understanding Chu's interpretation of *ming-te*.

32. *Ta-hsueh*, "Classic," par. 4.

33. *Li-chi chu-shu* 60.1b; cf. D. C. Lau, "A Note on Ke Wu," p. 353.

34. From the *Chang-chü* commentary on *Ta-hsueh*, "Classic," par. 4 (p. 138).

35. *Ta-hsueh*, "Commentary" V (the supplementary chapter of Chu Hsi).

36. Indeed, such a belief was central to the Ch'eng-Chu philosophical system. See, for example, Ch'eng I's comments in *I-shu*, p. 214 and p. 13, and in *I-ch'uan I-chuan* 3.3b. In *Yü-lei* 1.2a, Chu praises Ch'eng I's view.

37. Man's nature as principle is discussed in *Yü-lei* Chapters 4 and 5 passim.

38. In *Huo-wen* 33a-51a, Chu delineates the ideas in the supplementary chapter that are derived directly from Ch'eng I. Wing-tsit Chan, "Chu Hsi's Completion of Neo-Confucianism," p. 87, lists the passages in the *I-shu* that Chu Hsi drew upon in writing the supplementary chapter. I should point out, if it is at all necessary, that, although Chu "made bold to use the ideas of Ch'eng-tzu," it was Chu who fashioned these ideas into a coherent philosophical statement.

39. *Ta-hsueh*, "Commentary," V. As might be expected, from the moment the *Ta-hsueh chang-chü* began to circulate until the present day, serious questions have been raised about the authority of Chu's supplementary chapter. See note 56 to Chapter 3.

40. See Chu's preface to the *Ta-hsueh chang-chü,* "Ta-hsueh chang-chü hsu" 2b–3a (pp. 134–135).

41. *Yü-lei* 126, and Ch'ien Mu, *Chu-tzu hsin hsueh-an* III, 489–549 passim.

42. In *Yü-lei* 24.20b, Chu comments: "Of the outstanding men of our dynasty, there is not a one who has not been ensnared by Buddhism. These include men like Li Wen-ching, Wang Wen-cheng, Hsieh Shang-ts'ai, Yang Kuei-shan, and Master Yu [Tso]." Hsieh, Yang, and Yu are three of the so-called "Four Masters of the Ch'eng school." On Hsieh, Yang, and Yu's involvement in Ch'an, see Kusumoto Bun'yū, *Sōdai Jugaku no Zen shisō kenkyū,* pp. 286–325. Kano Naoki, *Chūgoku tetsugaku shi,* pp. 394–397, Morohashi Tetsuji, *Jugaku no mokuteki to Sō-ju no katsudō,* pp. 386–389, and Galen Sargent, *Tchou Hi contre le Bouddhisme,* pp. 26–27, 30, briefly discuss the Ch'engs' disciples and their contact with Buddhism.

43. The whole of *Yü-lei* 126 evidences profound concern over Buddhism's popular appeal. That Chu himself had been tempted by Buddhism (e.g., *Yü-lei* 104.9b–10a) no doubt added to his concern.

44. *Yü-lei* 126.10a. Elsewhere he says (*Wen-chi* 41.2a), "'Maintaining inner mental composure' and 'probing principle'—you cannot emphasize one and neglect the other."

45. *Yü-lei* 126.21a. Ch'eng Hao's statement is to be found in the *I-shu,* p. 153. Elsewhere Chu Hsi comments (*Yü-lei* 44.23b):

It is necessary to have learning on the lower level, only then can there be penetration on the higher level. Yet there are those who engage in learning on the lower level but are still unable to experience a penetration on the higher level—this is simply because their learning on the lower level is not adequate. If their learning on the lower level were adequate, they would necessarily experience a penetration on the higher level. The Buddhists speak only of penetration on the higher level; they pay no attention to learning on the lower level. But, if they pay no attention to learning on the lower level, how can they expect there to be penetration on the higher level?

46. *Ta-hsueh,* "Classic," par. 5.

47. The extent of Chu's "democratization" of the *Ta-hsueh* should not be exaggerated, however. He did indeed open up the text to a larger readership than that allowed for by earlier commentators. Theoretically, the self-cultivation process outlined there was now available to all. But Chu's *ko wu* was extremely demanding. Not everyone could engage in the lifelong struggle to apprehend the multitudinous manifestations of principle. One had to have the time to give to such a struggle; and one had to have the education necessary to pursue principle in the voluminous Classics and histories, where, according to Chu, it could be most readily apprehended. Hence, in practice, the self-cultivation proposed by Chu Hsi was limited largely to the educated elite.

Some three centuries later, Wang Yang-ming (1472–1529) and other thinkers of his philosophical school would more fully develop the "democratic" potential of the *Ta-hsueh.* Wang would understand *chih chih,* a central term in the *Ta-hsueh,* as "the extension of the innate faculty for knowing." This innate faculty for knowing—the ability possessed by all to distinguish right from wrong—would render the acquisition of knowledge superfluous to the process of moral self-perfection. Book-learning would no longer enhance the prospects of self-realization. Simply by bringing his behavior into line with his innate sense of right, any individual could readily perfect his virtue.

AN ANNOTATED TRANSLATION
OF THE *TA-HSUEH*
FOLLOWING CHU HSI'S READING

This book, the *Greater Learning*, explains the system by which people
were taught in the school for greater learning in ancient times.

Since heaven first gave birth to the people down below,[2] it has granted
them all the same nature of benevolence, righteousness, propriety, and wisdom.[3] Yet their psychophysical[4] endowments often prove unequal; so not
all are able to know the composition of their natures and thus to preserve
them whole. Should there appear among the people one who is bright and

---

The following abbreviation is used in the notes:

CC   *Ta-hsueh chang-chü* 大學章句 . *Ssu-pu pei yao* 四部備
要 ed. (Used to refer to Chu Hsi's commentary within the
Chang-chü; citations of CC are in every instance to Chu Hsi's comments specifically on the passage in question, and thus page references are not given.)

1. Chu Hsi rearranged the text of the "Ta-hsueh" chapter as it appeared
in the *Li chi*, divided it into 1 *ching* 經 chapter which he attributed to
Confucius and 10 *chuan* 傳 chapters which he attributed to Tseng Tzu,
commented upon it extensively, and appended to it the title *Ta-hsueh
chang-chü*, the *Greater Learning in Chapters and Verses*. The translation of
the *Ta-hsueh chang-chü* and its preface is based upon the *Ssu-pu pei-yao*
edition.

2. The phrase 天降生民 (*t'ien chiang sheng-min*) first appears in
Yang Hsiung's (B.C. 53–18) preface to the *Fa-yen, Yang-tzu fa-yen* 13.5a4.

3. Benevolence, righteousness, propriety, and wisdom as virtues common
to man's nature is a theme that appears throughout the *Meng-tzu;* see 2A/6,
6A/6, and 7A/21. Cf. James Legge, *Chinese Classics* II, 201–204; II, 401–
403, and II, 459–460.

4. 氣質 (*ch'i-chih;* "psychophysical") refers to one's psychic qualities
as well as material qualities and thus can be understood as "psychophysical
stuff."

wise,[5] capable of fulfilling the capacity of his nature, heaven would certainly ordain him to act as sovereign and instructor to the multitudes,[6] commissioning him to govern and teach them so that their natures be restored.[7]

Thus, Fu Hsi, Shen Nung, Huang Ti, Yao, and Shun[8] carried on for

---

5. The words 聰明睿智 (ts'ung-ming jui-chih) are found in *Chou i* 43/*Hsi* A/10 and *Chung-yung* 31/1. Cf. Z. D. Sung (with Legge translation), *The Text of Yi King: Chinese Original with English Translation*, pp. 297–298, and Legge, *Chinese Classics* I, 428.

6. The notion that heaven ordains sovereigns and instructors to guide the people first appears in *Shang shu* 11.6a, where we read: 天佑下民作之君作之師 .... Cf. Legge, *Chinese Classics* III, 286: "Now Heaven, to protect the inferior people, made for them rulers, and made for them instructors...." 下民 (hsia-min) should be translated here, "the people below," not "the inferior people."

7. In using the words 復其性 (fu ch'i hsing) here, Chu Hsi is clearly drawing on Li Ao's "Fu-hsing shu." Li Ao's influence on the Sung Neo-Confucians is noted by Fung Yu-lan, *History* II, 413–424. Also cf. Chu Hsi's commentary to *Lun-yü* 1/1 in *Lun-yü chi-chu* 1.1a4–5, where he says: 人性皆善，而覺有先後，後覺者必效先覺之所為乃可以明善而復其初也. "Man's nature is in all cases good, but, in discovering this goodness, there are those who lead and those who follow. Those who follow in discovering it must emulate the behavior of those who discover it first; only then can they understand their goodness and return to their original state."

8. Legendary rulers of China.

heaven[9] and established the highest point of excellence;[10] and these were the reasons[11] for which the office of the Minister of Education[12] and the post of the Director of Music[13] were founded.

Amidst the glory of the Three Dynasties,[14] regulations were gradually perfected, and thereafter schools were found everywhere, from the Imperial Palace and the state capitals on down to the villages. At the age of eight, all the male children, from the sons of kings and dukes to the sons of commoners, entered the school of lesser learning; there they were instructed in the chores of cleaning and sweeping, in the formalities of polite

---

9. The *locus classicus* of the term 繼天 (*chi-t'ien*) is the *Ku-liang chuan* 穀梁傳, where these words appear: ...繼天者,君也.君之所存者,命也. See *Ku-liang chuan* (in *Ch'un-ch'iu ching-chuan yin-te*), I, 205. Also cf. *Yang-tzu fa-yen* 13.5b7.

10. I.e., they established the highest point of excellence, which then served as the standard for those below them; thus (*chi*) might also be rendered as "norm," "standard." *Chi* as the "highest point of excellence" is first mentioned in *Shang shu* 12.11a where it is said: 皇建其有極敛時五福 . Cf. Legge, *Chinese Classics* III, 328: "The sovereign having established his highest point of excellence, he concentrates in himself the five happinesses. . . ." Also cf. Bernhard Karlgren, "Glosses on the *Book of Documents*," *Bulletin of the Museum of Far Eastern Antiquities* 20:232–233 (1948).

11. I.e., in order that they might "govern and teach them so that their natures be restored."

12. The responsibilities of the Minister of Education (司徒) are described in *Shang shu* 3.22a–b and 18.4a; cf. Legge, *Chinese Classics* III, 44 and III, 529.

13. The responsibilities of the Director of Music (典樂) are set forth in *Shang shu* 3.26a; cf. Legge, *Chinese Classics* III, 47–48. From the *Shang shu* accounts it may be observed that the function of both the Minister of Education and the Director of Music lay mainly in the area of instructing the people of the empire.

14. I.e., the Hsia, Shang, and Chou dynasties.

conversation and good manners,[15] and in the refinements of ritual, music, archery, charioteering, calligraphy, and mathematics.[16] At the age of fifteen, the Son of Heaven's eldest son[17] and other imperial sons on down to the eldest legitimate sons[18] of dukes, ministers, high officials, and officers of the chief grade,[19] together with the gifted from among the populace, all entered the school of greater learning;[20] there they were instructed in the Way of probing principle, setting the mind in the right, cultivating oneself,

---

15. Lit., "sprinkling and sweeping, answering and replying, and advancing and retreating." The *locus classicus* of the phrase 灑掃應對進退 (*shai-sao ying-tui chin-t'ui*) is *Lun-yü* 19/12; cf. Legge, *Chinese Classics* I, 343.

16. Referred to traditionally as the *liu-i* 六藝 (the six arts). See *Chou li* 19.24b; cf. Edouard Biot, *Le Tcheou-li,* Tome I, Livre ix, 213–214.

17. I.e., the heir-apparent.

18. 適子 (*shih-tzu*) is the same as 嫡子 (*ti-tzu*), meaning a son of the legal wife as opposed to that of a concubine.

19. The term 元士 (*yuan-shih*) refers to worthy officials under direct control of the king. Cf. *Li chi* 11.17b, where we read: 天子三公九卿二十七大夫八十一元士 . James Legge, *Li Ki (Sacred Books of the East,* XXVII), 213, translates, "The son of Heaven had three dukes, nine high ministers, twenty-seven Great officers, and eighty-one officers of the chief grade."

20. A similar passage appears in *Li chi* 13.2a: 王太子王子群后之大子卿大夫元士之適子國之俊選皆造焉凡入學以齒 . Legge's translation, *Li Ki,* p. 233, is as follows:

> The eldest son of the king and his other sons, the eldest sons of all the feudal princes, the sons, by their wives proper, of the high ministers, and officers of the highest grade, and the eminent and select scholars from [all] the states, all repaired [to their instruction], entering the schools according to their years.

and governing others.[21] This was the way instruction in the schools was divided into programs of greater and lesser learning.

Such was the scope of the establishment of schools; such too were the details of the sequence and program of instruction. As for the content of the instruction,[22] it was based entirely on principles drawn from the sovereign's personal experience and deep understanding,[23] and yet it consisted of nothing more than the standards of right conduct[24] to be followed by the people in their daily lives. Thus all in that age advanced in learning, and, in their advancement, they all came to know the primal constitution of their natures,[25] and at the same time, the duties that were demanded of each of them. Each man was diligent and put forth his utmost effort. This is why in the heyday

---

21. The terms 窮理 (ch'iung li), 正心 (cheng hsin), and 修己 (hsiu chi) all appear in the Ta-hsueh chang-chü; 治人 (chih jen) appears there as 治國 (chih kuo).

The view presented here that at 8 they entered the lower school and at 15 the advanced school accords with that presented in the Po-hu t'ung. See Po-hu t'ung te lun 4.16b5-7. For other theories about the ancients' educational system, as found in the Li chi, Shang shu ta-chuan 尚書大傳 etc., see the hsiao-hsueh 小學 entry in Morohashi Tetsuji, ed., Dai kanwa jiten Vol. IV, no. 7374 . . . 176.

22. More lit., "what was taken to constitute the instruction."

23. The locus classicus of the term 躬行 (kung-hsing; "personal experience") is found in Lun-yü 7/33. The locus classicus of the term 心得 (hsin-te; "deep understanding") is found in Chou i 11/15/2. The use of kung-hsing and hsin-te together is suggested by Meng-tzu 1A/7; cf. Legge, Chinese Classics II, 141.

24. The term 彞倫 (i-lun; "standards of right conduct") comes from Shang shu 12.2a; cf. Legge, Chinese Classics III, 320ff.

25. I.e., benevolence, righteousness, propriety, and wisdom. For the term 固有 (ku-yu), see Meng-tzu 6A/6: 仁義禮智非由外鑠我也我固有之也 . D. C. Lau, Mencius, p. 173, translates: "Benevolence, dutifulness, observance of the rites, and wisdom are not welded onto me from the outside; they are in me originally."

of antiquity good government flourished above and excellent customs prevailed below—it was a period never equaled by later generations.

As the Chou declined, worthy and sage sovereigns did not arise,[26] administration of schools was not kept up, education deteriorated, mores degenerated. Though a Sage like Confucius appeared in such times, he did not attain the position of sovereign-instructor, the position from which he could enact his politics and teachings. Alone, he took the ways of the former kings, recited and passed them on to his disciples, to proclaim them to later generations.

Chapters such as the "Ch'ü-li," "Shao-i," "Nei-tse,"[27] and "Ti-tzu chih"[28] originally were only ancillary writings[29] on lesser learning.[30] But this chapter [the "Ta-hsueh"] prominently sets forth the brilliant system of greater learning for those who have already completed the program of lesser learning: it develops the design of greater learning in all its magnitude and at the same time explores fully the details of the program of instruction.

---

26. Cf. *Meng-tzu* 2A/2: 賢聖之君六七作 . Legge, *Chinese Classics* II, 182 translates: "... there had appeared six or seven worthy and sage sovereigns."

27. "Ch'ü-li" 曲禮 comprises Chapters 1 and 2 of the *Li chi*, "Shao-i" 少儀 Chapter 17, and "Nei-tse" 內則 Chapter 12.

28. "Ti-tzu chih" 弟子職 is Chapter 59 of the *Kuan-tzu* 管子 .

29. Lit., "branches and fringes."

30. Chu Hsi suspected that historically there had existed a whole text concerning "lesser learning" but that it had become fragmented with the passage of time; see "T'i hsiao-hsueh" 題小學 in *Wen-chi* 76.21a3–10. A book entitled *Hsiao-hsueh* was compiled by Liu Ch'ing-chih (1130–1195) under Chu Hsi's direction, in which selections from the chapters mentioned here are included.

We may presume that every one of the three thousand disciples[31] heard this doctrine, yet only the tradition from the school of Tseng Tzu[32] had the full authority of it. The school thus wrote a commentary to bring out its meaning. With the death of Mencius the transmission ceased,[33] and, though the book was preserved, there were few who understood it. From then on, vulgar Confucians devoted twice as much effort to memorization and recitation,[34] and to the composition of ornate verse and essays[35] as they did to lesser learning, yet what they achieved was of no use. The

---

31. The "K'ung-tzu shih chia" 孔子世家 section of the *Shih chi* states that Confucius's disciples numbered three thousand; see *Shih chi* 47.75 where these words appear: 孔子以詩書禮樂,教弟子蓋三千焉 . E. Chavannes, *Les Mémoires historiques de Se-ma Ts'ien*, Tome V, Chapitre XLVII, p. 403 translates: "K'ong-tse prenait pour matière de son enseignment le *Che* (les Poésies), le *Chou* (les Documents historiques), les *Rites* et la *Musique*. Ses disciples doivent avoir été au nombre de trois mille."

32. For a short biography of this disciple of Confucius, see H. A. Giles, *A Chinese Biographical Dictionary*, pp. 768–769, no. 2022.

33. This complies with Han Yü's view that the transmission of the Way ceased with the death of Mencius. See "Yuan tao," *Ch'ang-li hsien-sheng wen-chi* 11.3b.

34. Memorization and recitation had been a prominent part of the examination system since the T'ang; cf. *Sung shih* 155.3b1–2. Chu Hsi here seems to be criticizing conventional or vulgar Confucians who, in their efforts to gain official position, devoted much time and energy to simple memorization.

35. Ornate verse and essays also had become an important part of the examination system; this may, in addition, be a reference to the over-aestheticism of the Sui, T'ang, and Sung Confucians, that is, their over-emphasis on belles-lettres.

heterodox teachings of emptiness and inaction,[36] of calmness and extinction[37] seemed "loftier" than great learning, yet they were without application to the real world. In addition, there appeared all manner of intrigues and strategems—that is, counsels designed to lead to great success and fame—together with the sects of the "hundred schools" and the "multitudinous experts,"[38] which confuse the world, deceive the people, and obstruct the path of benevolence and righteousness.[39] These caused the ruler misfortune, unable to hear the essentials of the Great Way; these caused the common people misfortune, unable to enjoy the best govern-

---

36. I.e., Taoism. The term 虛無 (*hsu wu*) is used to describe the technique of the Taoists as early as the *Shih chi;* see *Shih chi* 130.12–13, 其術以虛無為本以因循為用 . Burton Watson, *Ssu-ma Ch'ien: Grand Historian of China,* p. 47, translates this passage as follows: "Its teaching takes emptiness and inaction as its basis, and compliance and accordance [with nature and the times] as its practice."

37. I.e., nirvana, which, of course, is a reference to Buddhism. For the term 寂滅 (*chi-mieh*), see William Edward Soothill, *A Dictionary of Chinese Buddhist Terms,* p. 348.

38. E.g., divination, geomancy, physiognomy, military science, etc.

39. This phrase 惑世誣民充塞仁義 is similar to a passage in *Meng-tzu* 3B/9 where, in speaking of Yang Chu and Mo Ti, Mencius says: 楊墨之道不息孔子之道不著是邪說誣民充塞仁義也; cf. Legge, *Chinese Classics* II, 283, "If the principles of Yang and Mo be not stopped, and the principles of Confucius not set forth, then those perverse speakings will delude the people, and stop up [the path] of benevolence and righteousness."

ment.[40] Like a chronic disease, gloom and obstruction persisted,[41] until decay and chaos reached their peak with the end of the Five Dynasties.

Heaven moves in cycles: nothing goes that does not come back to its origins.[42] So the virtuous force of the Sung appeared in all its glory, and instruction flourished. At this time, the two Ch'eng brothers of Honan[43] appeared, and found it within their capacity to take up again the tradition of Mencius. Indeed, they were the first to give due honor to the *Greater Learning* and to make it known to the world;[44] and, after putting the text in order,[45] they explicated its essential points. Only then was the system of teaching employed in the school for greater learning in antiquity—

---

40. The term 至治 (*chih-chih;* "best government") comes from *Shang shu* 18.10b; cf. Legge, *Chinese Classics* III, 539.

41. The phrase 晦盲否塞，反覆沈痼 is reminiscent of much of the terminology found in the *Ts'an-t'ung-ch'i*, a Taoist book purportedly written by Wei Po-yang in A.D. 142. Indeed, Chu Hsi wrote a study of it entitled *Chou i ts'an-t'ung-ch'i k'ao-i* (Study of Variants in the Chou i ts'an-t'ung-ch'i), and thus was no doubt thoroughly familiar with its content and terminology. In particular, cf. Wei Po-yang, *Ts'an-t'ung-ch'i cheng-wen*, p. 18, where the 4 characters 眯冥否塞 appear.

42. The phrase 無往不復 (*wu-wang pu-fu*) is derived from *Chou i* 9/11/3; cf. Sung, *Yi King*, p. 57.

43. I.e., the brothers Ch'eng Hao (1032–1085) and Ch'eng I (1033–1107).

44. This refers to the fact that the Ch'eng brothers, following Ssu-ma Kuang's lead, lifted the "Ta-hsueh" chapter from the *Li chi* and treated it as an autonomous work; furthermore, they were the first to use the text in teaching disciples, making it "the gate through which beginning students enter into virtue." It is worth noting that Chu Hsi makes no mention of Ssu-ma Kuang here.

45. In antiquity, bamboo slips were tied together to form a volume (簡編). According to the Ch'eng brothers and Chu Hsi, the slips from the "Ta-hsueh" chapter in the *Li chi* had become disordered.

the subject of the Sage's Classic and the worthies' commentary[46]—brilliantly illuminated for the world again. Though I acknowledge my ignorance, I was still fortunate to have learned indirectly [from the Ch'eng brothers through their disciples and writings],[47] so share in having heard [the tradition].

Still, the text of the *Greater Learning* contained some errata and lacunae and hence, forgetting my rusticity, I edited it.[48] At times also I took the liberty of appending my own ideas and filling in the lacunae—these await [the criticism] of superior men of the future. I know full well that I have overstepped my bounds and that there is no way for me to escape blame. Yet, in explaining how the state should educate the people and perfect the customs, how the student should cultivate himself and govern others, this work need not be without some small benefit.

Preface done by Chu Hsi of Hsin-an on the *chia-tzu* day of the second month of the *chi-yu* year of the Ch'un-hsi period [20 February 1189].

---

46. I.e., Confucius's *ching* or Classic handed down by Tseng Tzu and Tseng Tzu's *chuan* or commentary recorded by his disciples.

47. Mencius uses the term 私淑 (*ssu-shu*) to describe his relationship to Confucius. See *Meng-tzu* 4B/22: 予未得為孔子之徒也予私淑諸人也 . Cf. D.C. Lau, *Mencius,* p. 132, where he translates: "I have not had the good fortune to have been a disciple of Confucius. I have learned indirectly from him through others." Chu Hsi seems to be suggesting that his relationship to the Ch'eng brothers is similar to that of Mencius to Confucius; he too was unable to hear the teachings directly from the masters themselves, but by means of their disciples and written works he was able to study their doctrines.

48. Lit., "gathered and compiled."

The masters[49] *Ch'eng-tzu*[50] *said, "The Greater Learning is a work handed down from Confucius; it is the gate through which beginning students enter into virtue. It is only through the preservation of this work that we can now see the sequence of the learning process among the ancients.* The Analects *and the* Mencius *should be read next. Students must follow this order in their studies; then they may approach the point where they are free from error."*[51]

---

49. 子 (*tzu*) before the surname here indicates that Chu Hsi regarded the Ch'eng brothers as his masters. The explanation of this practice of placing a *tzu* before the name of one's master first appears in the commentary to the *Kung-yang chuan* 3.7b.

In preparing this translation of the *Ta-hsueh*, I have benefited particularly from the following translations: Shimada Kenji, *Daigaku Chūyō;* Yamashita Ryūji, *Daigaku Chūyō;* Akatsuka Kiyoshi, *Daigaku Chūyō;* Morohashi Tetsuji, *Daigaku Chūyō;* and James Legge, *The Great Learning,* Vol. I of *The Chinese Classics.* I have consulted numerous other available Japanese, Chinese, and English translations of the text.

50. The quotation that follows is a paraphrase of two separate comments from the *Ho-nan Ch'eng-shih i-shu,* a collection of sayings of the Ch'eng brothers recorded by various disciples and compiled by Chu Hsi. According to the ascriptions in the *I-shu,* the first comment, which appears on p. 18, is that of Ch'eng Hao, while the second, which appears on p. 303, is that of Ch'eng I. Hence, in this context I have translated 子程子 (*tzu* Ch'eng-tzu) in the plural to refer to both brothers. It might be mentioned here that the name Ch'eng-tzu, in the writings of Chu Hsi, is frequently, but not always, a reference to both brothers. For a discussion of the *I-shu,* see Ts'ai, *The Philosophy of Ch'eng I,* pp. 29–37, and Graham, pp. 141–142.

51. The italics here are to signify that this is a comment by Chu Hsi.

1. The way of greater learning[52] lies in keeping one's inborn luminous Vir-

---

However, it is different from his commentary to the *Ta-hsueh* in that it has been traditionally treated as part of the Classic itself. Similarly, his comments that appear at the end of each chapter, together with his supplementary fifth chapter have, in effect, become part of the *Ta-hsueh* text. Thus, I have included them as part of the translation, italicizing them in every instance.

52. Whether the term 大學 (*ta-hsueh*) refers to great or extensive learning, learning for the great man, or learning for the adult is a problem unresolved by the various commentators. Cheng Hsuan and K'ung Ying-ta, authors of the commentary and subcommentary to the "Ta-hsueh" chapter in the *Li chi chu-shu*, interpret it as great or extensive learning, Wang Yang-ming as learning for the great man, and Chu Hsi as learning for the adult. In his commentary to the *Ta-hsueh* (hereafter cited simply as *CC*), Chu Hsi says: " 大學 (*ta-hsueh*) is 大人之學 (*ta-jen-chi hsueh*), learning for adults." Elsewhere, in the very first passage of his extremely important *Ta-hsueh huo-wen* 1a, we read: "You, my master, consider 大學之道 (*ta-hsueh chih tao*; the way of greater learning) to be 大人之學 (*ta-jen chih hsueh*). What is meant by that?' Chu Hsi responded, 'This is in contrast to 小子之學 (*hsiao-tzu chih hsueh*), "learning for children."'" And in his lecture to the Emperor on the *Ta-hsueh* in 1194, recorded in *Wen-chi* 15.1a–20b, Chu is quite explicit about the title:

大學 refers to 大人之學 . In the education of antiquity there was learning for children (小子之學), and learning for adults. Learning for children consisted in the chores of cleaning and sweeping, in the formalities of polite conversation and good manners, and in the refinements of ritual, music, archery, charioteering, calligraphy, and mathematics.

tue unobscured,[53] in renewing the people,[54] and in coming to rest in per-

---

Learning for adults consisted in the Way of probing principle, of cultivating the person, of establishing harmony in the household, of governing the state well, and of bringing tranquility to the empire. What this work treats is the learning for adults; hence it is named *Ta-hsueh*.

Also in his preface to the *Ta-hsueh chang-chü*, he gives an eloquent explanation of his views on the educational system of the ancients, where he again describes *ta-hsueh* as "learning for adults." Thus, I have rendered *hsiao-hsueh* as "lesser learning," that is, the more basic curriculum for children and *ta-hsueh* as "greater learning," the more advanced curriculum for adults.

53. Chu Hsi comments (*CC*):

明德 (*ming-te*; "inborn luminous Virtue") is what man acquires from heaven; it is unprejudiced, spiritual, and completely unmuddled and thereby embodies the multitudinous manifestations of principle and responds to the myriad affairs. But it may be restrained by the endowment of *ch'i* or concealed by human desire, so at times it will become obscured. Never, however, does its original luminosity cease. Therefore, the student should look to the light that emanates from it and seek to keep it unobscured, thereby restoring its original condition.

The similarity here to Buddhist terminology is noted in Chan, *Source Book*, p. 674, note 61. For a discussion of Chu Hsi's understanding of the term *ming-te*, see Chapter 4.

One is tempted to translate the first occurrence of *ming* here, that is the verb, "to keep bright" and to render the whole phrase *ming ming-te* something like "to keep the inborn luminous Virtue bright." However, "to keep bright" misses the philosophical point Chu Hsi is making. The *ming-te*, received by all, *never loses* its brightness or luminosity; rather, that brightness simply becomes obscured by human desire and *ch'i*. Thus, one does not strive to keep the Virtue bright, but to keep it unobscured.

54. Chu Hsi states (*CC*): "Ch'eng-tzu said, '親(*ch'in*; "to love") should be written as 新 (*hsin*; "to renew").'" This emendation is suggested by Ch'eng I in his arrangement of the *Ta-hsueh* in *Ho-nan Ch'eng-shih ching-*

fect goodness.[55]

2. Knowing where to come to rest,[56] one becomes steadfast; being steadfast,

---

shuo 5.3a2. In none of Chu Hsi's writings does there appear philological justification for the change from *ch'in* to *hsin;* when asked in *Huo-wen* 11a–b what sort of evidence exists for the emendation, he says that *ch'in min* makes little sense in the context and that the preferability of the *hsin min* alternative is attested to by the Tseng Tzu commentary. Chu Hsi further states in *CC:* "*Hsin* means 革其舊 (*ko ch'i chiu;* 'to remove the old'). It is said that, once one has personally kept one's inborn luminous Virtue unobscured, one must then extend it to others, so that they too might have the means to expel their 'long-stained impurities.'" The idea being expressed is that, once one has cultivated one's own inborn luminous Virtue—keeping it unobscured by human desire and *ch'i*—thereby restoring one's originally perfect condition, one then proceeds to bring about the same perfection in all other men. The use of 舊染之污 (*chiu-jan chih wu;* "long-stained impurities")️ is suggested by the occurrence of the words 舊染汙俗咸與惟新 (*chiu-jan wu su hsien yü wei hsin*) in *Shang shu* 7.13a; cf. Legge, *Chinese Classics* III, 168–179. ". . . those who have long been stained by filthy manners will be allowed to renovate themselves."

55. Chu Hsi says (*CC*): "It is stated that, both in keeping one's inborn luminous Virtue unobscured and in renewing the people, one ought to come to rest steadfastly in the place of perfect goodness." Although Chu Hsi also states in the commentary here that "these three items are the principia of the *Ta-hsueh*," it is clear that "coming to rest in perfect goodness" is not understood by Chu Hsi to be a third and separate endeavor, but rather a descriptive statement about how one should go about the first two items, "keeping the inborn luminous Virtue unobscured" and "renewing the people." See also *Yü-lei* 14.21b–22a.

56. Chu Hsi comments (*CC*): "止 (*chih*) is 所當止之地即至善之所在 (*so-tang chih chih ti chi chih-shan chih so-tsai;* 'the place where one ought to come to come to rest, namely, the place of perfect goodness')."

one may find peace of mind; peace of mind may lead to serenity; this serenity makes reflection possible; only with reflection is one able to reach the resting place.[57]

3. Things have their roots and branches [i.e., their fundamentals and what derives from them and depends on them];[58] affairs have a beginning and an end.[59] One comes near the Way in knowing what to put first and what to put last.[60]

4. Those of antiquity who wished that all men throughout the empire keep their inborn luminous Virtue unobscured[61] put governing their states well

---

57. Chu Hsi says (CC): "得 (te) means 得其所止 (te ch'i so-chih; 'to attain to the resting place')."

58. Chu Hsi states (CC): "'Keeping the inborn Virtue unobscured' constitutes the root; 'renewing the people,' the branch."

59. Chu Hsi comments (CC): "'Knowing where to come to rest' constitutes the beginning; 'being able to attain to the resting place,' the end."

60. About this paragraph Chu Hsi says (CC): "This passage sums up the preceding two paragraphs."

61. Chu Hsi comments (CC): 明明德於天下 (ming ming-te yü t'ien-hsia) means 使天下之人皆有以明其明德, 'to enable all men throughout the empire to keep their inborn luminous Virtue unobscured.'" This interpretation of the phrase differs from the traditional one found in K'ung Ying-ta's subcommentary to the Li chi version of the text (60.4a); Legge, who understands the passage according to K'ung's view, translates (*Chinese Classics* I, 357) "to illustrate illustrious virtue throughout the kingdom."

Chu Hsi assumes that he who is able to preserve his inborn luminous Virtue will extend his grace to others and thereby renew the people so that they too might be able to preserve their Virtue. He says in the *Ta-hsueh huo-wen* 13b:

What is meant by *ming ming-te yü t'ien-hsia* is "to keep one's inborn luminous Virtue unobscured, then to extend it to the people so as to renew them, enabling all men throughout the empire to keep their inborn luminous Virtue unobscured." If all men are capable of keeping

first; wishing to govern their states well, they first established harmony in their households; wishing to establish harmony in their households, they first cultivated themselves; wishing to cultivate themselves, they first set their minds in the right; wishing to set their minds in the right, they first made their thoughts true;[62] wishing to make their thoughts true, they first extended their knowledge to the utmost;[63] the extension of knowledge lies in fully apprehending the principle in things.[64]

> their inborn luminous Virtue unobscured, everyone will make his thoughts true, everyone will set his mind in the right, everyone will cultivate his person, everyone will treat his kinsmen as kinsmen, everyone will treat his elders as elders—so that throughout the empire all will be tranquil.

Thus, Chu's interpretation of this passage embraces the first two of the three principia, "keeping the inborn luminous unobscured Virtue" and "renewing the people." This, in turn, according to him, leads to the tranquilization of the empire; such a result is consistent with the next paragraph, which makes "bringing tranquility to the empire" the final of the eight steps.

62. Chu Hsi says (*CC*): "誠 (*ch'eng*) is 實 (*shih*; 'to make genuine or true')."

63. Chu Hsi says (*CC*): "致 (*chih*) is 推極 (*t'ui-chi*; 'to extend to the utmost'). 知 (*chih*) is similar to 識 (*shih*; 'knowledge'); *chih chih* is 'to extend our knowledge to the utmost with the desire that it become completely exhaustive.'"

64. Chu Hsi comments (*CC*): "格 (*ko*) is 至 (*chih*; 'to arrive at,' 'to reach'). 物 (*wu*) is similar to 事 (*shih*; 'affair'); *ko wu* is 'to reach to the utmost the principle in affairs and things with the desire that the extreme point always be reached.'" Chu Hsi comments that the 在 (*tsai*) here represents the extremely close connection between apprehending the principle in things and the extension of knowledge. When the principle in things has been apprehended, knowledge has already been extended, therefore the character 在, "lies in," is used. Unlike the relationship between the other items in this passage, there is no time lapse between these two. See *Yü-lei* 15.27a.

5. Only after the principle in things is fully apprehended does knowledge become complete; knowledge being complete, thoughts may become true; thoughts being true, the mind may become set in the right;[65] the mind

---

The *CC* also comments here: "These eight items are the particular steps 條目 of the *Ta-hsüeh*."

65. In this passage I translate only these two lines with a "may," for in *CC* Chu Hsi makes clear by glossing these lines alone that his understanding of them is different from that of the surrounding lines: "Knowledge being complete, the thoughts can then successfully be made true. The thoughts being true, the mind can then successfully be set in the right." In *Ssu-shu ta-ch'üan* 14b, Hu Ping-wen (1250–1333) lucidly explains that the reason for this gloss is to emphasize that, in these cases, one does not automatically advance from one step to the next but must continue to exert effort throughout. Cf. also Chu Hsi's comments at the end of *Ta-hsueh*, "Commentary," VI and VII, where he explains in some detail that progress from complete knowledge to true thoughts and from true thoughts to rectified mind is by no means inevitable but rather requires disciplined effort. In *Yü-lei* 16.38b and *Huo-wen* 56b, Chu Hsi argues a similar case for the relationship between setting the mind in the right and cultivation of the person. Although "may" then might be used here also, because the gloss in *CC* is specifically limited to the two lines, I have decided to limit the use of "may" in the present translation to those lines alone.

In *Yü-lei* 15.27b–28a, Chu Hsi offers a partial defense of his inconsistent treatment here of what is a grammatically parallel passage:

The *Ta-hsueh* speaks of 物格而后知至 on down through 天下平 . The Sage spoke broadly; he did not [specifically] say, if one is able to do this, one is then able to do that; nor did he say that, if one is able to do this, one can then study that. He just stated it broadly, as is. Later, chapter by chapter, paragraph after paragraph, further explanation is given. It's simply that men must come to an understanding of the passage on their own.

being so set, the person becomes cultivated; the person being cultivated, harmony is established in the household; household harmony established, the state becomes well-governed; the state being well-governed, the empire becomes tranquil.[66]

6. From the Son of Heaven on down to the commoners, all without exception[67] should regard self-cultivation as the root.

7. It is impossible that the root[68] be unhealthy and the branches healthy. Never should the important[69] be treated as trivial; never should the trivial be treated as important.

This, the Classic portion in one chapter, may be taken as the words of Confucius, transmitted by Tseng Tzu. The ten chapters of commentary contain the ideas of Tseng Tzu, recorded by his disciples. In the old version [of the Greater Learning*] there were passages out of place. Now, availing myself of Ch'eng-tzu's arrangement, and having reexamined the text of the Classic, I have ordered it as follows:*

---

66. Chu Hsi classifies the eight steps in the following manner (*CC*): "修身 (*hsiu shen*) on up [to 正心 (*cheng hsin*), 誠意 (*ch'eng i*), 致知 (*chih chih*) and 格物 (*ko wu*)] are the affairs of 'keeping the inborn luminous Virtue unobscured.' 齊家 (*ch'i chia*) on down [to 治國 (*chih kuo*) and 平天下 (*p'ing t'ien-hsia*)] are the affairs of 'renewing the people.'"

67. Chu Hsi comments (*CC*): " 壹是 (*i-shih*) is 一切 (*i-ch'ieh*; 'all', 'uniformly', 'without exception')." The sense is similar to that of the 皆 (*chieh*; 'all') that follows.

68. Chu Hsi states (*CC*): " 本 (*pen*; 'the root') refers to the person 身." According to *Huo-wen* 17a, the person, when spoken of in contrast to the empire, the state, and the household, is the root.

69. Chu Hsi says (*CC*): " 所厚 (*so-hou*; 'the important') refers to the household 家." *Huo-wen* 17a-b explains that, although the household, the state, and the empire are of the same principle, there nonetheless exists an order of importance among them.

Chapter I

1. In the "Announcement to the Prince of K'ang"[70] it is said, "[King Wen] was able to keep his Virtue unobscured."[71]

2. In the "T'ai-chia"[72] it is said, "[T'ang's] attention was constantly on[73] his heaven-given luminous Virtue."[74]

---

70. From the "Chou-shu" 周書 section of the *Shang shu*.

71. *Shang shu* 14.3a; cf. Legge, *Chinese Classics* III, 383 and Bernhard Karlgren, *The Book of Documents*, p. 39.

72. From the "Shang-shu" 商書 section of the *Shang shu*.

73. Chu Hsi comments (*CC*): "顧 (*ku*) means 常 目 在 之 (*ch'ang mu tsai chih*; 'constant attention was on it')."

74. This passage is found in *Shang shu* 8.18a; cf. Legge, *Chinese Classics* III, 199. Chu Hsi here equates 明命 (*ming-ming*) with 明德 (*ming-te*), saying, "From the point of view of man's receiving it, it is called *ming-te*; from the point of view of heaven it is called *ming-ming*" (*Yü-lei* 16.1a). In the *CC* it is stated: " 天之明命 (*t'ien chih ming-ming*) then is what heaven confers upon me as my inborn Virtue. If my attention is constantly on it, it will always be unobscured." See also *Yü-lei* 16.4a and *Ssu-shu ta-ch'üan* 20b–21a where Chu Hsi is quoted as saying: "It would seem that what heaven confers upon me is the *ming-ming*; what I acquire as my nature 性 is the *ming-te*." For Chu Hsi, then, it is simply the same concept viewed from two different perspectives. According to Chu Hsi (*Huo-wen* 21a-b), the luminous decree (*ming-ming*) received by man is the inborn luminous Virtue (*ming-te*). If he is constantly attentive to it, it will never become confused by human desires. Following his interpretation, I have translated *t'ien chih ming-ming* as "heaven-given luminous Virtue" rather than "the luminous decree of heaven," which is more literally what the Chinese says.

3. In the "Canon of Emperor Yao"[75] it is said, "He was able to keep his lofty Virtue unobscured."[76]

4. All [these passages speak of] keeping one's own inborn Virtue unobscured.[77]

This, the first chapter of commentary [by Tseng Tzu], explains "keeping the inborn luminous Virtue unobscured."

Chapter II

1. The inscription on T'ang's basin read, "If one day you truly renew yourself, day after day you should renew yourself; indeed, renew yourself every day."[78]

---

75. Chu Hsi states (*CC*): "'Ti-tien' 帝典 refers to the 'Yao-tien' 堯典 in the 'Yü-shu' 虞書 section [of the *Shang shu*]."

76. *Shang shu* 2.7b; Karlgren, *Documents,* p. 1 (with modification). Cf. Legge, *Chinese Classics* III, 17.

77. Chu Hsi comments (*CC*): "This sums up the citations from the *Shu ching;* [these passages] all refer to the idea of personally keeping one's own inborn Virtue unobscured."

78. Chu Hsi says (*CC*):

T'ang considered cleansing the mind to expel the evil to be similar to washing the body to expel the filth; that is why he so inscribed his basin. The inscription says that, if one day you are truly able to renew yourself by means of cleansing your "long-stained impurities" [see note 54], you ought to build upon what has already been renewed to renew yourself from day to day; indeed you ought to renew yourself every day—there mustn't be the slightest interruption.

For a more elaborate discussion of the inscription and the parallels between cleansing the mind and washing the body, see *Huo-wen* 22b–23b. Before one is able to renew the people, one must first renew oneself, that is, one must first keep one's inborn luminous Virtue unobscured (*Yü-lei* 16.4b).

2. In the "Announcement to the Prince of K'ang" it is said, "You shall give rise [79] to a renewed people."[80]

3. In the *Book of Poetry* it is said, "Though Chou is an old state, the charge it holds is new."[81]

4. For this purpose, the superior man exerts himself to the utmost in everything.[82]

This, the second chapter of commentary [by Tseng Tzu], elucidates "renewing the people."

Chapter III

1. In the *Book of Poetry* it is said, "The royal domain of a thousand *li* / Is where the people come to rest."[83]

---

79. Chu Hsi states (*CC*): "'To arouse them and to stir them up' is what is meant by 作 (*tso*)."

80. This is in *Shang shu* 14.5b; cf. Legge, *Chinese Classics* III, 388, and also Karlgren, *Documents*, p. 40. Chu Hsi explains his understanding of the line (*CC*): "The passage speaks of giving rise to a self-renewed people." Renewing oneself, by example, moves others to do the same (*Yü-lei* 16.4b–5a).

81. #235/1; cf. Bernard Karlgren, *The Book of Odes*, p. 185, and Legge, *Chinese Classics* IV, 427. Of this passage Chu Hsi says (*CC*), "Although the Chou state was old, it received the mandate of heaven for the first time with King Wen, who was able to renew his inborn Virtue and extend it to the people." According to *Yü-lei* 16.5a and *Huo-wen* 25b–26a, receiving the appointment is the natural result of renewing oneself and then the people.

82. Chu Hsi comments (*CC*), "Both in self-renewal and in renewal of the people he wishes to come to rest in perfect goodness."

83. #303/4; Legge, *Chinese Classics* IV, 637 (with slight modification). Cf. Karlgren, *Odes*, p. 263. According to Chu (*CC*), this passage "explains that each creature has a place where it ought to come to rest."

2. In the *Book of Poetry* it is said, "Min-man, the orioles sing[84]/ Resting on the peak's foliage."[85] The Master said, "They rest—and they know where to come to rest. Can a man be less than these birds?"[86]

3. In the *Book of Poetry* it is said, "Profound was King Wen/ Ah! continuously bright and deeply attentive—he came to rest [in perfect goodness]."[87] As a sovereign, he came to rest in benevolence; as a subject, he

---

84. Chu Hsi (*CC*) glosses 緡 蠻 (*min-man*) as 鳥聲 (*niao-sheng;* "the sound of the birds").

85. #230/2; cf. Legge, *Chinese Classics* IV, 418 and Karlgren, *Odes,* p. 182. Chu Hsi comments (*CC*): "丘 隅 (*ch'iu-yü*) is 岑 蔚 之 處 (*chen-wei chih ch'u;* 'the peak's foliage')."

86. Chu Hsi says (*CC*): "From 子 曰 (*tzu yueh;* 'The Master said') on down is Confucius's explanation of the ode, in which he says that man should know the spot where he ought to come to rest [i.e., perfect goodness]."

87. #235/4; cf. Legge, *Chinese Classics* IV, 429 and Karlgren, *Odes,* p. 186. Chu Hsi elaborates on the *Shih ching* phrase 緝 熙 敬 止 (*ch'i-hsi ching-chih*) in some detail in *Huo-wen* 27a:

> The multitude of men are dulled by their endowment of *ch'i* and their creaturely desires; therefore they are unable to be deeply attentive at all times and, accordingly, they miss the resting place [i.e., perfect goodness]. Only the mind of the sage, clear both inside and out, is not obstructed in the slightest. Therefore he is continuously bright and, naturally, deeply attentive at all times; accordingly, his resting place is always perfect goodness.

In addition to this statement, Chu Hsi comments in *CC,* "敬 止 (*ching-chih*) is to say that as he was always deeply attentive, he felt a natural ease wherever he came to rest." Although he understands *ching* here to mean "deeply attentive," in other contexts, such as the next sentence, he takes it to mean "reverence," the more common usage. Graham, pp. 68–69, explains these different semantic aspects of the term *ching:*

> . . . *ching* as it used in the *Analects* of Confucius, for example, is the attitude one assumes toward parents, ruler, spirits; it includes both the emotion of reverence and a state of self-possession, attentiveness, con-

came to rest in reverence. As a son, he came to rest in filial piety; as a father, he came to rest in affection. In intercourse with countrymen, he came to rest in fidelity.[88]

---

centration. It is generally translated 'respect' or 'reverence', but it is the other aspect which is the more prominent even in some passages of the *Analects*. . . .

The attitude which is assumed towards the parents and the spirits, collected, concentrated, free from muddle and distraction, is for the Ch'engs proof that the unity of mind can be maintained not only in contemplation, as Taoists and Buddhists suppose, but in action. It is the state of man when he is in full possession of himself—a state which in their opinion should be preserved at all times, although the ordinary man attains it only when he has to pull himself together for a special occasion. Thus *ching,* as the word is used by the Ch'engs and their successors, cannot be translated by "reverence". . . . The two aspects of *ching* are interdependent; to collect oneself, be attentive to a person or thing implies that one respects him or takes it seriously; and to be respectful implies that one is collected and attentive. But there is no English word which covers both, and the only course seems to be to use "reverence" for one and a different word for the other. . . .

Cf. also Chan, *Reflections on Things at Hand,* pp. 361–362, where he discusses these two aspects of *ching* in a similar manner. Chu Hsi's comments in both the *Huo-wen* and *CC* indicate clearly that in this instance he understands *ching* in the sense of the inner mental state of attentiveness.

As for the single character 止 (*chih;* "came to rest"), Chu Hsi acknowledges (*Huo-wen* 27a–b) that, as it originally appeared in the "Wen Wang" ode in the *Shih ching,* it was merely a final supplemental particle with no meaning; but, according to Chu, the ancients often quoted from the *Shih* in order to illustrate their own ideas without completely according with the original intent of the passage as it appeared in the *Shih.* And so, in the *Ta-hsueh, chih* became far more than the final particle it had been originally—it took on the substantive meaning of "come to rest," which indeed changed the gist of the entire line.

88. Chu Hsi says (*CC*), "The text cites this poem and explains that a sage's resting place is always perfect goodness."

4. In the *Book of Poetry* it is said,

> Look to the coves in the banks of the Ch'i
> With green bamboo, so lush and fine;
> There is our elegant and accomplished prince—
> As if cutting and filing,
> As if chiselling and polishing,
> [So he cultivates himself!]
> How grave is he and resolute!
> How commanding and distinguished!
> Our elegant and accomplished prince—
> Never can he be forgotten![89]

"As if cutting and filing" speaks to[90] the process of learning; "as if chiselling and polishing" to the process of self-cultivation.[91] "How grave is he

---

89. #55/1; Legge, *Chinese Classics* IV, 91 (with modification). Cf. Karlgren, *Odes,* p. 37. This poem, the "Ch'i-yü" 淇 奧 ode, praises Duke Wu of Wei; see Legge's note at the bottom of IV, 91.

90. Chu Hsi comments (*CC*), "道 (*tao*) is 言 (*yen,* 'to speak,' 'to refer')."

91. Cultivation of the person is likened here to the crafting of bone and horn, and jade and stone. Chu Hsi explains (*CC*):

> One cuts with a knife or a saw and chisels with a mallet or chisel to pare an object to a desired shape. One files with a rasp or a plane and polishes with sand or stone to give an object a smooth finish. In crafting bone and horn, one cuts then files repeatedly. In crafting jade and stone, one chisels then polishes repeatedly. Both of these cases show that in crafting an object there is a proper sequence according to which the object is brought to perfection.

In *Yü-lei* 16.6a it is said: "One cuts then files repeatedly, one chisels then polishes repeatedly—only then might one come to rest in perfect goodness. If one does otherwise, though one may [come to rest in] goodness, it is not perfect [goodness]." The idea expressed in both the *CC* and the *Yü-lei* passages is that, if one simply cuts but does not file, one does not come to rest in perfect goodness; likewise, if one chisels but does not polish, one does not come to rest in perfect goodness (*Yü-lei* 16.7a).

and resolute" involves a feeling of trepidation;[92] "how commanding and distinguished" is of an imposing demeanor.[93] "Our elegant and acomplished prince,—/ Never can he be forgotten" speaks to his abundant virtue and perfect goodness which the people cannot forget.[94]

5. In the *Book of Poetry* it is said, "Ah! the former kings[95] are not forgotten!"[96] Superior men [of later generations][97] have esteemed their worthiness and have treated their descendants with the affection due kinsmen. Commoners [of later generations] have delighted in the prosperity passed on by them and have profited from their benefactions.[98] Therefore, after

---

92. Chu Hsi makes these glosses (*CC*): "瑟 (se) is 嚴密之貌 (yen-mi chih mao; 'a grave bearing') and 僩 (hsien) is 武毅之貌 (wu-i chih mao; 'a resolute bearing') . . . 恂慄 (hsun-li) is 戰懼 (chan-chu; 'trepidation')." This apparent contradiction between a grave and resolute bearing and a feeling of trepidation is explained by Chu Hsi in *Yü-lei* 16.6b10–11: "A man filled with trepidation will necessarily be grave and stern. How could he transgress?"

93. According to Chu (*Huo-wen* 29a), the "feeling of trepidation" refers to a cautious reverence being maintained within, the "imposing demeanor" to a brilliance being manifested without.

94. Chu Hsi says (*CC*): "The text cites this poem and explains it in order to illustrate 'the coming to rest in perfect goodness' of one who 'keeps one's inborn luminous Virtue unobscured.'"

95. Chu Hsi comments (*CC*): "前王 (ch'ien-wang; 'former kings') refers to Kings Wen and Wu."

96. #269/3; Legge, *Chinese Classics* IV, 573. Cf. Karlgren, *Odes*, p. 241.

97. *Chün-tzu* (superior men) here, according to Chu Hsi, is a reference to both moral and political leaders. He says (*CC*): "君子 (chün-tzu; 'superior men') refers to [both] worthies and kings of later generations."

98. K'ung Ying-ta's paraphrase in *Li chi* 60.6a presents a different interpretation:

Superior men of later generations have admired the former kings' ability to treat their worthy men as worthy and their kinsmen with the affection due kinsmen. . . . Humble commoners of later generations have

coming to the end of their days they have not been forgotten.[99]

---

admired the former kings' ability to delight in what delighted the people . . . and to find profit in what profited the people.

In the *Ta-hsueh tsuan-shu* 39b, Chu Hsi is quoted as saying: "As for 親 (*ch'in*), 賢 (*hsien*), 樂 (*le*), and 利 (*li*), the first appearance of each is spoken of from the point of view of the men of later generations, while the second appearance of each refers in some cases to the former kings' persons and in some cases to their benignities." It is clear then that, according to Chu, the four occurrences of 其 (*ch'i*) in this passage all refer to the former kings. This point is emphasized by Ts'ai Hsu-chai (1453–1508) in Abei Bōzan *Shisho kummō shūso* 1.27b.

Chu Hsi's understanding of this passage is more fully expressed in *Yü-lei* 16.7b1–2:

Somebody inquired about the line "Superior men [of later generations] have esteemed their worthiness and have treated their descendants with the affection due kinsmen." Chu Hsi responded, "For example, Confucius looked up with respect to the virtue of Wen and Wu; this is 'to esteem their worthiness.' [Kings] Ch'eng and K'ang on down, grateful for their [i.e., Wen and Wu's] kindness, protected their legacy; this then is 'to treat their descendants with the affection due kinsmen.'"

It should be noted that, elsewhere in the *Yü-lei,* Chu Hsi understands this passage differently. In 16.7a he takes 賢其賢 in the sense of 賢其所賢 and 親其親 in the sense of 親其所親: "Superior men [of later generations] have esteemed those whom they esteemed and have held dear those whom they held dear." But, since this view is presented in Chu's works far less frequently, I have translated according to the other version. Yamashita, Akatsuka, and Shimada, in their translations of Chu's understanding of the *Ta-hsueh,* all read the passage as I do.

For an interesting discussion of both of Chu Hsi's interpretations, see Ts'ai Hsu-chai's *Ssu-shu meng-yin* 2.11b–12b.

99. Chu Hsi comments (*CC*):

This, the third chapter of commentary [by Tseng Tzu], elucidates "coming to rest in perfect goodness."

Chapter IV

1. "The Master said, 'In hearing litigations, I am no different from others.[100] But what is necessary is to create conditions where there are no litigations.'"[101] Then those whose accusations are baseless will not be able to pour out all their lies—so greatly shall the people's will be kept in awe.[102] This is called "knowing the root."[103]

This passage states that, in renewing the people, the former kings came to rest in perfect goodness, enabling every single creature then in the realm, as well as those of later generations, to attain to their proper places. Thus, even after the former kings came to the end of their days, men yearned for them—though more time elapse, still they will not be forgotten.

100. Chu Hsi states (*CC*): " 猶人 (*yu jen*) is 不異於人 (*pu-i yü jen;* 'to be no different from others')."

101. *Lun-yü* 12/13; cf. Legge, *Chinese Classics* I, 257 and Arthur Waley, *The Analects of Confucius*, p. 167.

102. Chu Hsi explains (*CC*):

This passage cites the words of the Master then explains that a sage is able to bring it about that persons whose accusations are baseless dare not pour out all their lies. It seems that, once his inborn luminous Virtue becomes unobscured, he naturally is capable of awing into submission the people's will. Consequently, litigations will disappear of their own accord, without ever being heard.

And in *Yü-lei* 16.8a5–6 Chu remarks:

"Those whose accusations are baseless will not be able to pour out all their lies" explains the reason there will be no litigations. But first one must be capable of bringing into submission the people's will—in this way one is able to prevent them from pouring out all their lies.

See also *Huo-wen* 30b–31a.

103. According to Chu Hsi (*Yü-lei* 16.8a4), "'to create conditions where

This, the fourth chapter of commentary [by Tseng Tzu], elucidates "the roots and the branches."

Chapter V

1. This is called "knowing the root."[104]
2. This is called "the completion of knowledge."[105]

It would appear that the preceding, the fifth chapter of commentary [by Tseng Tzu], elucidated the meaning of "fully apprehending the principle in things" and "the extension of knowledge," but it is now lost. Recently, I made bold to use the ideas of Ch'eng-tzu to supplement it as follows: what is meant by "the extension of knowledge lies in fully apprehending the principle in things" is that, if we wish to extend our knowledge to the utmost, we must probe thoroughly the principle in those things we encoun-

---

there are no litigations' is a matter that rests with the individual, it is the 'root'; if one looks at it like this, 'hearing litigations' is the 'branch.'" Chu defines the root in this particular context as "creating conditions where there are no litigations"—the ability to do this, according to him, ultimately depends upon the individual's keeping his luminous Virtue unobscured. For then, "he naturally is capable of awing into submission the people's will. Consequently, litigations will disappear of their own accord, without ever being heard." This is consistent with Chu Hsi's comment on "Classic," par. 3 (note 58): "'keeping the inborn Virtue unobscured' constitutes the root."

104. Chu Hsi states (CC): "Ch'eng-tzu said, 'This is superfluous text 衍文 .'" Ch'eng I makes this comment in *Ho-nan Ch'eng-shih ching-shuo* 5.3b6.

105. Chu Hsi comments (CC): "Above this line there is a hiatus in the text 闕文 ; this is merely the concluding phrase."

ter. It would seem that every man's intellect is possessed of the capacity for knowing and that every thing in the world is possessed of principle. But, to the extent that principle is not yet thoroughly probed, man's knowledge is not yet fully realized. Hence, the first step of instruction in greater learning is to teach the student, whenever he encounters anything at all in the world, to build upon what is already known to him of principle and to probe still further, so that he seeks to reach the limit. After exerting himself in this way for a long time, he will one day become enlightened and thoroughly understand [principle]; then, the manifest and the hidden, the subtle and the obvious qualities of all things will all be known, and the mind, in its whole substance and vast operations, will be completely illuminated. This is called "fully apprehending the principle in things." This is called "the completion of knowledge."

Chapter VI

1. "Becoming true in one's thoughts" is allowing no self-deception[106]—as one hates the hateful smell, as one loves the lovely color.[107] And this in

---

106. Chu Hsi says (*CC*): "What is meant by 'self-deception' (自 欺) is that one may know to practice good and expel evil but what issues forth from the mind [i.e., the thoughts] still contains that which is not true." And, in explaining the idea of "self-deception" in *Yü-lei* 16.12b: "It may be likened to something that is silver on the outside and iron on the inside—this is 'self-deception.' It is necessary for the outside and the inside to be the same—this is to be 'without self-deception.'" And again in *Yü-lei* 16.12b: "Outwardly doing good things but inwardly in fact feeling quite different is 'self-deception.' It may be compared to a piece of copper that is coated with gold on the outside—inside it is not true gold."

107. Chu Hsi remarks (*CC*):

It is said that, once he who wishes to cultivate himself knows to practice

turn means that one may keep one's self-respect.[108] Therefore, the superior man will always be watchful over himself when he is alone.[109]

2. The petty man, when alone, practices evil, stopping at nothing. But, as soon as he sees the superior man, he draws back and disguises himself, concealing evil and making a display of good. If, when others look at him, it is as though they see his [very] lungs and liver—of what benefit [is the disguise]?[110] This is called what is true within being manifested without. Therefore, the superior man will always be watchful over himself when he is alone.

3. Tseng Tzu said, "It will be seen by ten eyes, pointed at by ten hands. How awesome!"[111]

---

good and expel evil, he then must truly make the effort to prevent self-deception so that his hatred of evil will be as [natural as] the hatred of a hateful smell and his love of good will be as [natural as] the love of a lovely color.

108. According to Chu Hsi (CC), the 謙 (ch'ien) of 自謙 (tzu-ch'ien) should be read 慊 (ch'ieh), and means "to be pleased, satisfied." Being careful always to expel evil and to practice good, he is satisfied with his own person and does not accord with the expectations of others in violation of principle.

109. For 慎獨 (shen-tu) cf. Chung-yung 1/3, Legge, Chinese Classics I, 384. Chu Hsi explains (CC) that whether one's thoughts are true or untrue is not perceptible to other men but to oneself alone; consequently one must be ever-watchful over oneself.

110. Chu Hsi comments (CC):

It is said here that the petty man secretly practices evil but wishes to conceal it outwardly. It is not, then, that he does not know that good ought to be practiced and evil expelled; it is only that he is unable truly to make the effort and so arrives at such a condition. And still, he wishes to conceal his evil but in the end cannot; he wishes to pretend to practice good but in the end cannot. Of what benefit then [is the disguise]?

111. Chu Hsi says (CC): "This is cited in order to illustrate the meaning

4. As wealth enriches the house, so virtue enriches the person; [for with virtue] the mind will be magnanimous and the body relaxed. It is for this reason that the superior man must make his thoughts true.

This, the sixth chapter of commentary [by Tseng Tzu], elucidates "making the thoughts true."[112]

Chapter VII

1. What is meant by "the cultivation of the person depends upon setting

---

of the preceding passage. It explains that, even if one be in seclusion, such is the inconcealability of one's good and evil. Awe-inspiring indeed!"

112. It is worth quoting James Legge's *Chinese Classics* I, 367 comment on this chapter:

> It is only the first of these paragraphs from which we can in any way ascertain the views of the writer on making the thoughts sincere. The other paragraphs contain only illustration or enforcement. Now the gist of the first paragraph seems to be in 毋自欺 , "allowing no self-deception." After knowledge has been carried to the utmost, this remains to be done, and it is not true that, when knowledge has been completed, the thoughts become sincere.

Chu Hsi too is aware of the effort required to make the thoughts true, even after knowledge has been made complete (*CC*): ". . . there are some [whose minds are] already illuminated but who are not solicitous about making the thoughts true; and so what had been illuminated will again be lost to them and they will have no way to build a foundation for entering into virtue." Legge goes on to intimate that Chu Hsi's interpretation of the related passage in the Classic portion of the text ("Classic," par. 5) misses this point. But as I have tried to show in the translation of that passage and in note 65, Chu Hsi is aware that the step "thoughts becoming true" does not spontaneously follow upon the completion of knowledge.

the mind in the right" is this: neither in rage, nor in terror, nor in doting, nor in misery can the mind[113] achieve its right balance.[114]

2. If the mind is not present [i.e., attending], one looks but does not see, listens but does not hear, eats but does not appreciate the flavor.[115]

3. This is what is meant by "the cultivation of the person depends upon setting the mind in the right."

This, the seventh chapter of commentary [by Tseng Tzu], elucidates "setting the mind in the right" and "cultivation of the person."[116]

---

113. Chu Hsi here follows Ch'eng I's emendation of the text (*CC*): "Ch'eng-tzu said, '身 (*shen*) of 身有 (*shen yu*) should be written (*hsin*).'" See *Ho-nan Ch'eng-shih ching-shuo* 5.4a.

114. Chu Hsi remarks (*CC*):

It would seem that these four things [i.e., rage, terror, doting, and misery], being operations of the mind, are familiar to everyone. But, if once under their influence a person is unable to keep close watch over them, desires (欲) will be aroused and the emotions (情) will prevail. Thus, in some cases, the effect of these operations will be a loss of the right balance.

115. Chu Hsi explains this passage (*CC*):

If the mind is not preserved, there is no means by which the person (身) may be regulated. Hence, the superior man will always keep watch over the mind; through his attentiveness he will maintain its correctness [敬 以直之 is derived from *Chou i* 4/2/*Wen-yen*; cf. Sung, *Yi King*, pp. 20-21]. Then, the mind will at all times be preserved and the person completely cultivated.

116. Chu Hsi emphasizes here that, once the thoughts have been made true, additional effort is still needed to set the mind in the right (*CC*):

It would seem that, the thoughts having been made true, there would in fact be no evil and there would in truth be good; hence, one would be able to preserve one's mind and thereby regulate one's person. Yet, there are those who only know to make their thoughts true but are unable to keep close watch over the preservation of their minds; and so

Chapter VIII

1. What is meant by "establishing harmony in the household depends upon the cultivation of the person" is this: men are biased[117] in favor of[118] what they hold dear; biased against what they despise; biased in favor of what they revere; biased in favor of what they pity; and biased against what they scorn. Therefore, under heaven there are few who love something and yet appreciate its faults, who hate something and yet appreciate its virtues.[119]

2. Hence, as the proverb says, "No one recognizes his son's evils, and no one recognizes the full ear in his sprout of grain."[120]

3. This is what is meant by "if one's person is not cultivated, one cannot establish harmony in the household."

This, the eighth chapter of commentary [by Tseng Tzu], elucidates "cultivation of the person" and "establishing harmony in the household."

---

they are incapable of maintaining their inner correctness and of cultivating their persons.

117. Chu Hsi comments (*CC*): "辟 (*p'i*) is similar to 偏 (*p'ien;* 'biased,' 'one-sided')."

118. Chu Hsi understands (*CC*) the 之 (*chih*) that appears here and at the beginning of each of the following lines as 於 (*yü;* "in regard to"); rather than throughout the passage translating "biased in regard to," I have translated "biased in favor of" or "biased against," depending upon the context.

119. Chu Hsi comments (*CC*) that these five things (i.e., holding dear, despising, and so forth) are natural to man. Yet, when such emotions are allowed to go unchecked and become excessive (cf. *Yü-lei* 16.35a ff.), they will lead him into a trap of one-sidedness. In which case, of course, cultivation of the person is impossible. Cf. note 114.

120. Chu Hsi says (*CC*): "One who is enamored will not be clear-headed; one who is greedy will be insatiable. These are the ill effects of bias and the reasons for which harmony is not be established in the household."

Chapter IX

1. What is meant by "to govern the state well, it is necessary first to establish harmony in the household" is this: no one is able to teach others who cannot teach his own household. Therefore, the superior man does not leave his household yet his teachings are accomplished throughout the state. Filial piety becomes the means to serve the ruler; fraternal respect becomes the means to serve the elders; parental kindness becomes the means to treat the multitude. [121]

2. In the "Announcement to the Prince of K'ang" it is said, "[Deal with the people] as if you were taking care of an infant." [122] Though you may not hit the mark exactly, if you try sincerely in your heart, you will not be far off. There has never been a woman who would marry only after studying how to rear a child. [123]

3. If one household is humane, the whole state will be stirred to a sense of

---

121. Chu Hsi states (*CC*):

One's person being cultivated, one's household can be taught. Filial piety, fraternal respect, and parental kindness are the means whereby one cultivates oneself and what one teaches to one's household. In the state the way of serving the ruler, serving the elders, and treating the multitude consists of nothing more than these [three things]. For this reason, once household harmony is established above, the teachings will be accomplished below.

In *Yü-lei* 16.39b, Chu Hsi comments that filial piety, fraternal respect, and parental kindness are practiced by one's family; people throughout the state see these principles being displayed and are able themselves to practice them. It is not therefore that one actively seeks to extend these teachings from one's family to the state at large. This idea that filial piety, fraternal respect, and parental kindness influence the people of the state essentially through their moral power is expressed several times in *Yü-lei* 16.39b–40a.

122. *Shang shu* 14.6b; Legge, *Chinese Classics* III, 389 (with some modification). Cf. Karlgren, *Documents,* pp. 39–41.

123. The gist of this passage according to Chu Hsi (*Yü-lei* 16.40a and

humaneness; if one household is courteous, the whole state will be stirred to a sense of courtesy. If the One Man[124] is avaricious and perverse, the whole state will be led to rebellious disorder. Such are the springs of action.[125] This is what is meant by "One word may ruin the affairs [of state];[126] the One Man may put the state in order."[127]

4. Yao and Shun led the empire with benevolence, and the people followed their example; Chieh and Chou led the empire with violence, and the people followed their example. If what one decrees for others is contrary to what one loves oneself, the people will not obey.[128] Hence, only

---

Huo-wen 57b) is that the ruler should treat the multitude with the same kindness a parent instinctively feels toward his child (慈).

124. Chu Hsi says (CC): " 一人 (i-jen; 'the One Man') refers to the ruler." Cheng Hsuan and K'ung Ying-ta both gloss (Li chi 60.8b and 60.13b-14a) both 一家 and 一人 as "the ruler"; that Chu, by contrast, glosses only the 一人 would seem to indicate that his understanding of 一家 differs from theirs. Hence I have translated it here as "one household."

125. Chu Hsi comments (CC): "機(chi) is 'that where the activity originates.'"

126. Cf. Lun-yü 13/13; Legge, Chinese Classics I, 268-269.

127. Chu Hsi says (CC) that this line speaks of "the positive results of the teachings having been accomplished throughout the state."

128. The idea expressed here is a typically Confucian one: the power of moral example. That is, the people are transformed by the moral example of their ruler: if he is benevolent, they will become benevolent and refuse to obey all but benevolent orders; if he is violent, they will become violent and refuse to obey all but violent orders. An alternative reading of this sentence might be: "What the latter two decreed for others was contrary to what they cherished themselves so the people did not obey." Grammatically and contextually this is a justified reading. However, Chu Hsi's understanding of the line in CC is in the more general sense (see note 129). Such a general interpretation does indeed seem preferable for a number of reasons: the aphoristic nature of the line would suggest a broad reading;

after the superior man possesses goodness himself will he demand it of others; only after he is himself free of evil will he condemn it in others. No one has ever been able to teach others unless he himself was able to put himself in the position of those others.[129]

5. Therefore, governing the state well depends upon establishing harmony in the household.

6. In the *Book of Poetry* it is said:

> The peach tree is young and elegant;
> Luxuriant are its leaves.
> This young lady is going to her future home,
> And will order well her household.[130]

Only after ordering one's own household well can one teach the people of the state.

7. In the *Book of Poetry* it is said, "May relations between their brothers

---

the two　　in the line need not refer only to Chieh and Chou; and most important, as I have suggested, the line makes better contextual sense as it now reads.

129. Chu Hsi explains (*CC*):

When there is good in oneself, one can then demand good in others; when there is no evil in oneself, one can then rectify the evil in others. In both of these cases, one puts oneself in the position of others; this is what is called 恕 (*shu*), "the principle of reciprocity." If one does not do so, then what one decrees for others will be contrary to what one loves oneself and the people will not obey.

For further discussion of this passage, see *Huo-wen* 58a–60b; in 58b Chu Hsi explains that the character 恕 (*shu*) has the meaning of its components 如 (*ju*) and 心 (*hsin*): "Regulate others as (如) with the heart (心) that regulates oneself. Love others as (如) with the heart (心) that loves oneself."

130. #6/3; Legge, *Chinese Classics* IV, 13 (with slight modification). Cf. Karlgren, *Odes*, p. 5.

be as they should be!"[131] Only after relations between one's brothers are as they should be can one teach the people of the state.

8. In the *Book of Poetry* it is said, "There is no fault in his behavior/ Thus all the state is in its right balance."[132] Only when one is a worthy model as father, son, elder brother, and younger brother, will the people model themselves after him.

9. This is what is meant by "governing the state well depends upon establishing harmony in the household."

This, the ninth chapter of commentary [by Tseng Tzu], elucidates "establishing harmony in the household" and "governing the state well."

Chapter X

1. What is meant by "bringing tranquility to the empire depends upon good governance of the state" is this: when the ruler treats the aged of his own family in a manner befitting their venerable age[133] the people will be stirred to a sense of filial piety; when in his own family the ruler treats those who are older than himself in a manner befitting their elderly status the people will be stirred to a sense of fraternal respect; when the ruler takes pity on the young and fatherless the people will not be disobedient.[134]

---

131. #173/3; Legge, *Chinese Classics* IV, 275 (with modification). Cf. Karlgren, *Odes,* p. 117.

132. #152/3; cf. Legge, *Chinese Classics* IV, 223, and Karlgren, *Odes,* p. 95.

133. Chu Hsi says (CC): " 老老 (lao lao) is the so-called 老吾老 (lao wu-lao) [of *Meng-tzu* 1A/7]." D. C. Lau, *Mencius,* p. 56, translates the phrase 老吾老 : "Treat the aged of your own family in a manner befitting their venerable age."

134. Chu Hsi comments (CC): "It is said that the ruler practices these three things and as quick in reply as a shadow or an echo the subjects follow his example. This is what is meant by 'household harmony being established, the state becomes well-governed.'"

To bring this about, the ruler must follow the principle of the "measuring-square"—having the proper measure in one's own mind to measure the minds of others.[135]

2. In dealing with subordinates, do not practice what you hate in your superiors; in serving superiors, do not practice what you hate in your subordinates. In leading those behind you, do not practice what you hate in those ahead of you; in following those ahead of you, do not practice what you hate in those behind you. In intercourse with those on your left, do not practice what you hate in those on your right; in intercourse with those on your right, do not practice what you hate in those on your left. This is what is called the principle of having the proper measure in one's own mind to measure the minds of others.[136]

---

135. Chu Hsi glosses (CC) 絜 (hsieh) as 度 (tu; "to measure"), and 矩 (chü) as 所以為方 (so-i wei fang; "an instrument for squaring"). In Yü-lei 16.44a, he understands chü to refer to one's mind and explains the principle of 絜矩 (hsieh-chü) as follows: "The superior man perceives that the minds of others and his own are similar. Hence he always uses his own mind to measure the minds of others, so that all will become tranquil." He expresses this idea numerous times in Yü-lei 16.43a–46b.

The close connection between 恕 (shu) of "Commentary," IX.4, and 絜矩 (hsieh-chü) here is demonstrated by Chu Hsi's comment in Yü-lei 16.47b: "恕 (shu) also is the meaning of 絜矩 (hsieh-chü)."

136. Chu Hsi elaborates (CC) somewhat on what has often been called the Chinese version of the Golden Rule by giving some examples:

If you do not wish your superiors to be discourteous toward you, dare not treat your subordinates with discourteousness—be mindful of how you feel in measuring their minds. If you do not wish your subordinates to be disloyal toward you, dare not serve your superiors with disloyalty—be mindful of how you feel in measuring their minds.

Chu comments (CC) that "this paragraph explains the meaning of the two characters 絜矩 (hsieh-chü) in the above passage."

3. In the *Book of Poetry* it is said, "You are to be rejoiced in, O prince/ Father and mother to the people."[137] What the people love he loves; what the people hate he hates. This is called being father and mother to the people.[138]

4. In the *Book of Poetry* it is said:

> Lofty is that southern hill,
> With its masses of rocks!
> Awe-inspiring are you, O [Grand-] master Yin,
> And the people all look to you![139]

Whoever has charge of the state must take care, for, if he shows partiality, he will be a disgrace in the eyes of the world.[140]

---

137. #172/3; Legge, *Chinese Classics* IV, 273 (with modification). Cf. Karlgren, *Odes,* p. 116.

138. Chu Hsi says (*CC*) of this passage: "It explains that, able to measure the minds of others, he takes the mind of the people as his own—this is to love the people as his children, in which case the people will love him as father and mother." Cf. the last line of *Meng-tzu* 1B/7.

139. #191/1; Legge, *Chinese Classics* IV, 309. Cf. Karlgren, *Odes,* p. 133.

140. Chu Hsi says (*CC*):

> This passage explains that he in high position is looked up to with respect; he must take care. If he is unable to measure the minds of others and his loves and hates are guided by his own personal inclinations [alone and not by the loves and hates of the people], he will himself be slain, his kingdom will perish, and he will become a great disgrace in the eyes of the world (身弒國亡為天下之大戮矣).

Meng-tzu 4A/2 contains the phrase 身弒國亡 (*shen shih kuo wang*) which Legge translates in II, 293: "[He] will himself be slain, and his kingdom will perish."

The character 戮 (*lu*) in the commentary, which is used to define 僇 (*lu*) in the text, can mean either "to disgrace" or "to kill." I have chosen to translate it here as "disgrace" for the following reason: Chu Hsi's com-

5. In the *Book of Poetry* it is said:

When the rulers of Yin had not yet lost the multitude,
They were able to be a counterpart to Shang Ti. [141]
Observe closely [142] the fate of Yin;
The great Mandate is not easy to keep. [143]

This implies that to gain the multitude is to gain the state, to lose the multitude is to lose the state. [144]

6. Therefore, the ruler puts watchfulness over his (inborn luminous) Virtue first. [145] In having the (luminous) Virtue [146] he will have the people with

---

mentary is virtually a verbatim citation of *Hsun-tzu* 7.4a which reads 身死國亡為天下大僇. The T'ang dynasty commentator Yang Liang glosses the last part of this phrase as: 為天下大僇辱也. Therefore, despite the ambiguity of the character 僇 (*lu*) in Chu's comment, if we follow Yang Liang's commentary, with which Chu Hsi was no doubt familiar, we may feel confident that Chu intended the 僇 in his statement to be understood in the sense of "to disgrace" rather than "to put to death." Contextually also this reading is more appropriate, for, once a ruler has been slain, it makes little sense to have him killed again.

141. Chu Hsi comments (*CC*): "配上帝 (*p'ei shang-ti*) means 'acting as the rulers of all under heaven, they corresponded to Shang Ti.'"

142. Chu Hsi glosses (*CC*) 監 (*chien*) as 視 (*shih*; "to observe closely").

143. #235/6; cf. Karlgren, *Odes*, p. 186 and Legge, *Chinese Classics* IV, 431. Chu comments (*CC*): "不易 (*pu-i*) means 難保 (*nan-pao*; 'difficult to keep')."

144. Asked about the meaning of this line, Chu Hsi replies in *Huo-wen* 65a:

If the ruler is able to measure the minds of others, the people will regard him as father and mother and he will thereby gain the multitude and gain the state. If the ruler is unable to measure the minds of others, he will become a disgrace in the eyes of the world and so lose the multitude and lose the state.

145. Chu Hsi makes (*CC*) this gloss: "德 (*te*; 'Virtue') is the so-called 明德 (*ming-te*; 'the inborn luminous Virtue')."

146. The reader should be reminded that, according to Chu Hsi, all men

him;[147] and with the people, territory,[148] and with territory, wealth, and with wealth, resources for expenditure.

7. (The inborn luminous) Virtue is the root; wealth is the branch.

8. But, should the ruler regard the root as secondary and the branch as primary, he will contend with the people and teach them to plunder.[149]

9. Therefore, when wealth is gathered the people disperse; when wealth is dispersed the people gather.[150]

10. Therefore, words uttered by the ruler in a manner contrary to right

---

are possessed of the inborn luminous Virtue; but each man must make deliberate and continuous effort to keep it unobscured (the object of the self-cultivation process). "Having the luminous Virtue" here refers specifically to having successfully kept the inborn luminous Virtue unobscured.

147. Chu Hsi comments (CC): "有人 (yu jen; 'to have the people with him') refers to 得眾 (te chung; 'to gain the multitude') [cf. "Commentary," X.5]."

148. Chu Hsi comments (CC): "有土 (yu t'u; lit., 'to have the territory') refers to 得國 (te kuo; 'to gain the state' [cf. "Commentary," X.5]."

149. Chu Hsi explains (CC) 施奪 (shih to) as 施之以劫奪之教 (shih chih i chieh-to chih chiao; "to propagate among them the teachings of plunder") or, less literally, "to teach them to plunder." Chu concludes his commentary on this passage as follows:

It seems that wealth is something all men desire; if the ruler, unable to measure the minds of others, wishes to monopolize the wealth, the people will rise up and contend for plunder.

150. Chu Hsi remarks (CC):

He regards the root as secondary and the branch as primary, therefore wealth is gathered; he contends with the people and teaches them to plunder, therefore they disperse. If he reverses this [i.e., regards the root as primary and the branch as secondary], he will have the (luminous) Virtue and, thus, have the people with him [cf. "Commentary," X.6].

come back to him in a manner contrary to right; wealth come to him by means contrary to right leaves him by means contrary to right.[151]

11. In the "Announcement to the Prince of K'ang" it is said, "The Mandate of Heaven is not constant."[152] That is to say, when the ruler is good he obtains it,[153] when he is not good he loses it.[154]

12. In the *Book of Ch'u*[155] it is said, "The state of Ch'u treasures no object; it treasures only good men."[156]

---

151. In *Huo-wen* 65b, Chu Hsi expresses agreement with Cheng Hsuan's interpretation of the passage which says that, when the ruler's orders are contrary to right, the people's response will be the same. And when the ruler is avaricious, his subjects will encroach upon the property of others.

Chu Hsi comments (*CC*) that from "Commentary," X.6 to the end of this passage the subject of wealth is discussed as a means of illustrating the relative success and failure of those able and unable to measure the minds of others.

152. *Shang shu* 14.13b; cf. Legge, *Chinese Classics* III, 397 and Karlgren, *Documents,* p. 43.

153. Chu Hsi comments in *Huo-wen* 65b: "It seems that 'when he is good he obtains it' is a way of saying 'having the (luminous) Virtue, he will have the people with him' [cf. 'Commentary,' X.6]."

154. Chu Hsi again comments in *Huo-wen* 65b: "'When he is not good he loses it' is a way of saying 'What comes to him by means contrary to right leaves him by means contrary to right' [cf. 'Commentary,' X.10]."

Chu Hsi says (*CC*) that this passage is a further discussion of "Commentary," X.5.

155. According to Chu Hsi (*CC*), the *Book of Ch'u* refers to the *Ch'u yü* found in the *Kuo yü.*

156. Chu Hsi glosses (*CC*) 善 (*shan*) as 善人 (*shan-jen*), "good men."

This passage is probably an allusion to *Kuo yü* 18.10a6–10 where a Ch'u envoy to Chin 晉 is asked how long Ch'u's famous white girdle-pendant has been considered a treasure. He replies that in Ch'u it has never been considered a treasure; what Ch'u treasures instead is Kuan She-fu, a worthy official.

13. [Ch'ung-erh's] Uncle Fan said, "Our fugitive prince treasures no object; he treasures only love[157] of kin."[158]

14. In the "Speech of the Duke of Ch'in"[159] it is said:

> Let me have but one minister, sincere and devoted, without other abilities; a man whose mind is broad and upright and possessed of generosity; who esteems the talents of others as if he himself possessed them; and who, upon finding accomplished and sage-like men, loves them in his heart more than his speech expresses, truly showing himself able to accept them. Such a minister would be able to preserve my descendants and my people. Would that I might have such a benefit.[160]

> But a minister who, upon finding men of ability, is jealous and hates them, who upon finding accomplished and sage-like men, opposes them and does not allow their advancement, showing himself really not able to accept them—such a man will not be able to protect my descendants and people, and furthermore will be dangerous.[161]

---

157. Chu glosses (CC) 仁 (jen) as 愛 (ai; "to love").

158. Ch'ung-erh 重耳 is the personal name of the son of Duke Hsien of Chin, who was later to become Duke Wen. Uncle Fan is his maternal uncle whose personal name is Hu Yen (tzu Tzu Fan). Ch'ung-erh was slandered by his father's favorite concubine and consequently fled the state of Chin. Duke Hsien died, whereupon Duke Mu of Ch'in sent a messenger to Ch'ung-erh advising him to take the opportunity to seize control of Chin. Ch'ung-erh reported this to his Uncle Fan who gave the reply we have in the text. For this account, see the "T'an-kung" section of the Li chi (9.8b–10a) and Legge's translation in Li Ki, pp. 165–167. Cf. also Giles, Biographical Dictionary, p. 209, no. 523.

159. From the "Chou-shu" section of the Shang shu.

160. Where the Shang shu reads 亦職有利哉 (i chih yu li tsai) the Ta-hsueh reads 尚亦有利哉 (shang i yu li tsai). Chu glosses (CC) 尚 (shang) as 庶幾 (shu-chi; "would that there might").

161. Shang shu 20.13a–14a; Legge, Chinese Classics III, 629–630 (with modification). Cf. Karlgren, Documents, p. 81.

15. Only the humane man will banish such a jealous man, driving him out among the barbarian tribes beyond the four borders. He will not dwell together with him in the Middle Kingdom.[162] This is what is meant by "only the humane man is able to love others and to hate others."[163]

16. It is negligence[164] to see a worthy man but not to raise him to office or to raise him to office but not to do so at once.[165] Likewise, it is a mistake to see an evil man but not to remove him from office or to remove him from office but not to do so to a distant region.

17. To love what men hate or to hate what men love goes against human nature.[166] One who does so will surely meet with calamity.[167]

---

162. Lit., "he will not share the Middle Kingdom with him."

163. This is a paraphrase of *Lun-yü* 4/3, where we read: 子曰唯仁者能好人能惡人 . Cf. Legge, *Chinese Classics* I, 166 and Waley, *Analects*, p. 102.

Chu Hsi comments (*CC*):

> This passage explains that if there exist such jealous (娼疾) men who hinder the worthy and thereby injure the state, they will be intensely disliked and bitterly renounced by the humane man. Because he is completely disinterested and unselfish (至公無私), the humane man is able to achieve impartiality in his loves and hates.

164. Chu Hsi comments (*CC*): "As for 命 (*ming*), Cheng Hsuan says that it should be written 慢 (*man*), and Ch'eng I says that it should be written 怠 (*tai*). I have yet to determine who is correct." Cf. *Huo-wen* 66b–67a. Here I have translated according to Ch'eng I, although *man* too has somewhat the sense of "negligence."

165. In *Yü-lei* 16.49a, Chu Hsi says: "先 (*hsien*) means 早 (*tsao;* 'early,' or 'soon'); [the phrase] means 不能速用 (*pu-neng su yung;* 'to be unable to employ him promptly')."

166. Chu Hsi says (*CC*), "To love good and to hate evil is human nature."

167. Chu Hsi remarks (*CC*) that the "Speech of the Duke of Ch'in" in "Commentary," X.14 through the end of this passage elucidates the meaning of odes #172 and #191 cited in "Commentary," X.3 and X.4.

18. Thus, there is a great course[168] to be followed by the ruler:[169] to gain the multitude he must be true to his nature[170] and true to others;[171] through arrogance and wantonness he will lose it.[172]

19. There is a great course to be followed in the generation of wealth: let producers be many and consumers few; let production be speedy and expenditure unhurried.[173] Then wealth will always be sufficient.[174]

---

168. The "course" (道) is described by Chu Hsi (*CC*) as "the art of cultivating himself and governing others while occupying the position [i.e., the throne]."

169. According to Chu (*CC*), 君子 (*chün-tzu*) is spoken of here with reference to position (位); thus "ruler" or "sovereign" is intended rather than "superior man."

170. Chu Hsi glosses (*CC*) 忠 (*chung*) as 發己自盡 (*fa chi tzu chin;* "to manifest and give full development to oneself"). In *Huo-wen* 67a, it is glossed as 盡己之心 (*chin chi chih hsin;* "to develop fully one's mind"). Cf. Chan's comment on *Lun-yü* 4/15 in *Source Book,* p. 27, and also Legge's translation of the same passage in *Chinese Classics* I, 170, where *chung* is rendered "to be true to the principles of our nature."

171. (*hsin*) is explained by Chu Hsi (*CC*) as 循物無違 (*hsun wu wu wei;* "never to break an agreement with others"); see *Mathews' Chinese-English Dictionary,* no. 2926.9.

172. Chu Hsi says (*CC*), "This passage accords with the ideas in the 'Wen Wang' ode and the 'Announcement to the Prince of K'ang' quoted above ('Commentary,' X.5 and X.11)." Thus 得之 (*te chih*) here should be understood as 得眾 (*te chung;* "to gain the multitude"), or 得國 (*te kuo;* "to gain the state"). Cf. *Yü-lei* 16.49b1–4.

173. Chu Hsi quotes (*CC*) Lü Ta-lin 呂大臨 (1044–1093), a disciple of the Ch'eng brothers:

When the country is without vagrants, producers will be many; when the court is without positions for favorites, consumers will be few; when the time proper for farming is not taken away from the people, production will be speedy; when spending is regulated by the amount of income, expenditure will be unhurried.

174. Chu Hsi argues (*CC*) that this passage accords with the idea 有土

20. The humane man disperses his wealth and thereby distinguishes himself (i.e., gains the people); the inhumane man destroys himself that he might increase his wealth.[175]

21. Never has a ruler loved humaneness without his subordinates loving righteousness. Never have they loved righteousness without completely fulfilling their duties. Never in such a state has the wealth stored in the treasury soon departed.[176]

有財 , "having the territory, he will have wealth" in "Commentary," X.6. According to him, the passage explains that the way to enrich the country lies in being attentive to the root ("Commentary," X.7), that is, the luminous Virtue, and frugal in spending; it is not necessary "to regard the root as secondary and the branch [i.e., wealth] as primary" ("Commentary," X.8) to amass wealth.

175. Chu Hsi explains (*CC*): "The humane man disperses his wealth, thereby gaining the people. The inhumane man ruins himself to increase his wealth." In *Huo-wen* 68a, he further explains: "The humane man is not selfish about his possessions, therefore his wealth disperses, the people gather round him, and he is esteemed. The inhumane man desires only profit, therefore he sacrifices his life (捐身) and invites calamity in order to increase his wealth." Cf. "Commentary," X.9.

176. Chu Hsi explains (*CC*):

When a ruler is fond of humanity and thereby loves those under him, those under him will be fond of righteousness and so serve their ruler loyally. Consequently, they will always fulfill their duties; never then will the wealth in the treasury "leave by means contrary to right" [cf. 'Commentary,' X.10].

Also *Huo-wen* 68a: "When the duties are completely fulfilled, the ruler will be secure, rich, and honored [cf. *Meng-tzu* 7A/32; Lau, *Mencius,* p. 189] and the wealth in the treasury may be preserved for a long time (府庫之財可長保矣)." The last part of the final sentence in the text of "Commentary," X.21 has been translated according to Chu Hsi's sentiments expressed in the above two passages.

22. Meng Hsien-tzu [177] said,

> He who keeps a team of four horses [178] does not tend to fowl and pigs. The household that uses ice [in funeral rites and sacrifices] [179] does not keep cattle and sheep. The household of one hundred chariots [180] does not keep a minister who collects excessive revenue from the people—rather than such a man it would be better to have a minister who pilfers the household treasury. [181]

This is what is meant by "a state gains by righteousness and not by interest in gain."

23. The head of a state or household who makes wealth and its expenditure his chief cares is certain to be under the influence of petty men. . . . [182] If

---

177. Chu Hsi identifies (CC) Meng Hsien-tzu as "the worthy officer from the state of Lu, Chung-sun Mieh." He appears in the *Tso chuan*; see, in particular, Legge's notes on V, 271 and 304.

178. According to Chu Hsi (CC), "he who keeps a team of four horses" refers to one who has just become a great officer (大夫).

179. Chu Hsi glosses (CC) "the household that uses ice": "Ministers and great officers on up use ice in funeral rites and sacrifices."

180. Chu says (CC) that "the household of one hundred chariots" refers to the household that controls a fiefdom.

181. Chu Hsi explains (CC): "The superior man would rather lose his own wealth than bear sapping the people of their strength. Hence he would rather have a minister who pilfers [from him] than one who collects excessive revenue from the people." In *Huo-wen* 69a, Chu Hsi depicts the "minister who collects excessive revenue" as one who strips the people of their blood and fat; the "minister who pilfers" as one who steals from the ruler's treasury. The former case, Chu argues, is disastrous for the people, while the latter is not.

182. 自 of 自 小 人 (*tzu hsiao-jen*) is glossed by Chu Hsi (CC) as 由 (*yu*), "because of," "owing to." 自 小 人 is explained by Chu as 自 小 人 導 之 (*yu hsiao-jen tao chih*), "because of petty men guiding

petty men are employed in governing the state or household, calamity and misfortune together will result. And, though there be an able man,[183] he will be of no avail. This is what is meant by "a state gains by righteousness and not by interest in gain."

This, the tenth chapter of commentary [by Tseng Tzu], elucidates "governing the state well" and "bringing tranquility to the empire."

There are, in all, ten chapters of commentary [by Tseng Tzu], the first four of which discuss in general terms the gist of the principia,[184] the latter six of which discuss in detail the effort required in each of the particu-

---

him." In other words, when rulers treasure wealth, it is invariably "because petty men guide them."

As for the four characters 彼為善之 (*pi wei shan chih*) which follow in the text (and which are represented in the translation by the ellipsis), Chu Hsi says (*CC*), "I suspect there are omissions and mistaken characters above and below this phrase." In *Ho-nan Ch'eng-chih ching-shuo* 5.5b, Ch'eng I suggests the following emendation of the text: 彼為不善之小人使之為國家 ".... If such petty men who practice evil be employed in governing the state or household...." Chu does not mention this emendation in his commentary here or in his writings elsewhere; we may assume from this that, in this instance, he rejects Ch'eng I's reading. He apparently also discounts the traditional views of Cheng Hsuan and K'ung Ying-ta which appear in *Li chi* 60.12b and 19a. Because Chu Hsi is of the opinion that these four characters do not make sense as they now stand and because he offers no alternative reading, the phrase is left untranslated here.

183. In *Yü-lei* 16.50a, Chu Hsi explains 善 (*shan*) as 會 (*hui;* "able"). Thus 善者 should be understood as "the able man" and not "the good man." If Chu were to leave the *shan* here unglossed, *shan-che* would be read in its ordinary sense, "the good man." But this reading would pose a contradiction to what Chu feels is implied throughout the *Ta-hsueh,* that one perfectly virtuous man can bring tranquility to the entire empire.

184. I.e., the 三綱領, keeping the inborn luminous Virtue unobscured, renewing the people, and coming to rest in perfect goodness.

lar steps.[185] *The fifth chapter contains what is essential for "understanding goodness," and the sixth what is fundamental in "making oneself true."*[186] *These two chapters deal with especially urgent matters that demand the attention of the beginning student. The reader should not neglect them on account of their simplicity.*[187]

---

185. I.e., the 八條目 , fully apprehending the principle in things, extending knowledge to the utmost, making the thoughts true, setting the mind in the right, cultivating the person, establishing harmony in the household, governing the state well, and bringing tranquility to the empire.

186. For the terms "understanding goodness" (明善) and "making oneself true" (誠身), cf. *Chung-yung* 20/17, where we read 不明乎 善不誠乎身矣 , which Legge I, 413 translates, "If a man do not understand what is good, he will not attain sincerity in himself." Also cf. *Meng-tzu* 4A/12.

187. For the character 近 (*chin;* "simplicity") cf. *Meng-tzu* 7B/32, where the characters 言近 (*yen chin*) appear, translated by Legge II, 494 "words which are simple."

The preceding, the *Greater Learning,* with a Classic portion of two hundred and five characters and a commentary of ten chapters, may presently be found in Tai [Sheng's] book on rites;[189] but the text there is in disarray and the commentary has to some degree lost its proper order. Master Ch'eng-tzu corrected the *Greater Learning;* without considering my ability, I have ventured to rearrange the text, following his views.[190] Now, the first chapter of commentary elucidates "keeping the inborn luminous Virtue unobscured"; the second chapter, "renewing the people"; the third chapter, "coming to rest in perfect goodness";[191] the fourth chapter "the roots and the branches"; the fifth chapter, "the extension of knowledge";[192] the sixth chapter, "making the thoughts true";[193] the seventh chapter, "setting the mind in the right" and "cultivation of the person"; the eighth chapter, "cultivation of the person" and "establishing harmony in the household"; and the ninth chapter, "establishing harmony in the household," "governing the state well," and "bringing tranquility to the empire."[194] There is a natural order to the work, and the ideas are all

---

188. The "Postscript" appears in *Wen-chi* 81.9a–b.

189. I.e., Tai Sheng's version of the *Li chi.* See Chapter 2, "The *Ta-hsueh* Before Chu Hsi," p. 24.

190. As I have already discussed in Chapter 2, both Ch'eng Hao and Ch'eng I revised the *Ta-hsueh* text; their versions may be found in *Ho-nan Ch'eng-shih ching-shuo* 5.1a–5b. Chu Hsi follows Ch'eng I's revisions, it seems, exclusively; therefore I have translated 子程子 (*tzu* Ch'eng-tzu) in the singular here.

191. In commentary interspersed in the text here, Chu Hsi says, "All of the above chapters accord with Ch'eng's edition but I have added [to them the portion] from 'In the *Book of Poetry* it is said, "Look to the coves in the banks of the Ch'i"' on down."

192. Chu Hsi comments, "Both these chapters are present arrangements."

193. Chu Hsi says, "This accords with Ch'eng's edition."

194. Chu Hsi comments, "All these chapters accord with the older ver-

interrelated; it would seem that I have reconstructed the original form of the text. I have respectfully recorded it above in its proper order. The superfluous passages and the mistaken characters, which the former worthy [Ch'eng I][195] corrected, are all preserved [in the text] in their original form; I have placed circles above them and noted the corrections. These corrections together with my present doubts concerning the text may be found in my commentary.

Respectfully, Chu Hsi of Hsin-an.

---

sion [i.e., *Li chi* version]." Here in the postscript he seems to conflate what are "Commentary," IX and X in his *Chang-chü*. In the *Chang-chü* he says that the ninth chapter "elucidates 'establishing harmony in the household' and 'governing the state well' and that the "Commentary," X "elucidates 'governing the state well' and 'bringing tranquility to the empire.'" It may be that the division into 10 chapters of commentary instead of 9 was a revision he made sometime after the postscript was written and that he never returned to the postscript to correct it.

195. Although both brothers revised the order of the *Ta-hsueh*, Ch'eng I alone corrected what he believed to be superfluous or mistaken characters; he placed these corrections in notes accompanying the passage in question. See *Ho-nan Ch'eng-shih ching-shuo* 5.3a–5b.

CHINESE TEXT OF THE

TA-HSUEH CHANG-CHÜ

AND THE ''CHI TA-HSUEH HOU''

The Ta-hsueh chang-chü (The Greater Learning in chapters and verses) found in the *Ssu-pu pei-yao* edition of the *Ssu-shu chi-chu* is reproduced here. Chu Hsi's commentary is presented in full for the interested Sinologist, although it is translated only selectively in the footnotes to "An Annotated Translation of the *Ta-hsueh* Following Chu Hsi's Reading."

"Chi Ta-hsueh hou" (Postscript to the Greater Learning), also reproduced here, is from *Hui-an hsien-sheng Chu Wen-kung wen-chi* (*Ssu-pu ts'ung-k'an* ed.), 81.9a–b.

大學章句序

大學之書古之大學所以教人之法也蓋自天降生
民則既莫不與之以仁義禮智之性矣然其氣質之
禀或不能齊是以不能皆有以知其性之所有而全
之也一有聰明睿智能盡其性者出於其閒則天必
命之以為億兆之君師使之治而教之以復其性此
伏羲神農黃帝堯舜所以繼天立極而司徒之職典
樂之官所由設也三代之隆其法浸備然後王宮國
都以及閭巷莫不有學人生八歲則自王公以下至
於庶人之子弟皆入小學而教之以灑掃應對進退

之節禮樂射御書數之文及其十有五年則自天子
之元子眾子以至公卿大夫元士之適子與凡民之
俊秀皆入大學而教之以窮理正心脩己治人之道
此又學校之教大小之節所以分也夫以學校之設
其廣如此教之之術其次第節目之詳又如此而其
所以為教則又皆本之人君躬行心得之餘不待求
之民生日用彝倫之外是以當世之人無不學其學
焉者無不有以知其性分之所固有職分之所當為
而各俛焉以盡其力此古昔盛時所以治隆於上俗
美於下而非後世之所能及也及周之衰賢聖之君

珍倣宋版印

不作學校之政不脩教化陵夷風俗頹敗時則有若
孔子之聖而不得君師之位以行其政教於是獨取
先王之法誦而傳之以詔後世若曲禮少儀內則弟
子職諸篇固小學之支流餘裔而此篇者則因小學
之成功以著大學之明法外有以極其規模之大而
內有以盡其節目之詳者也三千之徒蓋莫不聞其
說而曾氏之傳獨得其宗於是作為傳義以發其意
及孟子沒而其傳泯焉則其書雖存而知者鮮矣自
是以來俗儒記誦詞章之習其功倍於小學而無用
異端虛無寂滅之教其高過於大學而無實其他權

大學序

二 中華書局聚

謀術數一切以就功名之說與夫百家眾技之流所
以惑世誣民充塞仁義者又紛然雜出乎其間使其
君子不幸而不得聞大道之要其小人不幸而不得
蒙至治之澤晦盲否塞反覆沈痼以及五季之衰而
壞亂極矣天運循環無往不復宋德隆盛治教休明
於是河南程氏兩夫子出而有以接乎孟氏之傳實
始尊信此篇而表章之既又為之次其簡編發其歸
趣然後古者大學教人之法聖經賢傳之指粲然復
明於世雖以熹之不敏亦幸私淑而與有聞焉顧其
爲書猶頗放失是以忘其固陋采而輯之閒亦竊附

珍倣宋版印

己意補其闕略以俟後之君子極知僭踰無所逃罪。
然於國家化民成俗之意學者脩己治人之方則未
必無小補云淳熙己酉二月甲子新安朱熹序

大學序

三 中華書局聚

大學 大舊音泰 今讀如字

朱熹章句

子程子曰大學孔氏之遺書而初學入德之門
也於今可見古人爲學次第者獨賴此篇之存
而論孟次之學者必由是而學焉則庶乎其不
差矣

大學之道在明明德在親民在止於至善 程子曰親當作新 ○

大學者大人之學也明明之也明德者人之所得乎
天而虛靈不昧以具衆理而應萬事者也但爲氣稟
所拘人欲所蔽則有時而昏然其本體之明則有未
嘗息者故學者當因其所發而遂明之以復其初也
新者革其舊之謂也言既自明其明德又當推以及
人使之亦有以去其舊染之污也止者必至於是而
不遷之意至善則事理當然之極也言明明德新民
皆當止於至善之地而不遷蓋必其有以盡夫天理

大學

中華書局聚

4.　3.　2.

之極。而無一毫人欲之私
也。此三者大學之綱領也。
知止而后有定定而后能

后與後同。○

静静而后能安安而后能慮慮而后能得
止者所當止之地卽至善之所在也。知之則志有定
向靜謂心不妄動安謂所處而安慮謂處事精詳得
謂得其所止。

所謂止得其

物有本末事有終始知所先後則近道矣
明德為本。新民為末。知止為始。能得為終。本始所先。末終所後。此結上文兩節之意。

古之欲明明

德於天下者先治其國欲治其國者先齊其家欲齊
其家者先脩其身欲脩其身者先正其心欲正其心
者先誠其意欲誠其意者先致其知致知在格物

者先誠其意者使天下之人皆有以

明德於天下者誠實也意者心之所

發也。知猶識也。推極吾之知識欲其所知無不盡也。推

137

大
學

格至也物猶事也窮至事物之理欲其
極處無不到也此八者大學之條目也物格而后知

至知至而后意誠意誠而后心正心正而后身脩
脩而后家齊家齊而后國治國治而后天下平聲治後去
之放此○知無不盡者物理之極處無不到也知至者吾心
之所知無不盡也知既盡則意可得而實矣意既實則心可
下則新民之事也物格知至則知所止矣意誠以下則皆
身壹是一切以下則舉此而錯之耳脩身以上明明德之事也齊家以
之皆得所止之序也自天子以至於庶人壹是皆以脩身爲本
之皆得所止之序也正心以上皆所以脩身也齊家以

否矣其所厚者薄而其所薄者厚未之有也本謂身所厚
上謂文家兩節之意此兩節結謂文家也此兩節結
身也是一切以下則舉此而錯之耳其本亂而末治者

右經一章蓋孔子之言而曾子述之凡二百
五字二百
二中華書局聚

I.4　　I.3　　　　I.1–2

其傳十章則曾子之意而門人記之也舊本

頗有錯簡今因程子所定而更考經文別爲

序次如左　凡傳文雜引經傳若無統紀然文○凡傳接文續雜血
脈貫通深淺始終至爲精密熟
讀詳味久當見之今不盡釋也

康誥曰克明德　康誥周書克能也

大甲曰顧諟天之明命　讀大
此作泰誓或曰古是字也○大甲商書顧謂常目在之也諟猶此也或曰審也○天之明命卽天之所以與我而我之所以爲德者也常目在之則無時不明矣

帝典曰克明峻德　帝典堯典虞書峻書作俊○

皆自明也　書峻大也○結所引書皆言自明己德之意

右傳之首章釋明明德　此通下三章至此爲止信舊本誤在沒世不忘之

下忘之

湯之盤銘曰。苟日新。日日新。又日新。銘盤銘。名其器之盤以自也。

警之辟也。湯以人之洗濯其心以去惡如沐浴其身以去垢。故銘其盤言誠能一日有以滌其舊染之污而自新則當因其已新者而日日新之又日新之不可略有間斷也。

康誥曰。作新民。鼓之舞之之謂作言振起其自新之民也。

詩曰。周雖舊邦。其命維新。大詩言周國雖舊而始受天命至於文王是故君子無所不用其極。止自新新民皆欲止於至善也。

右傳之二章釋新民。

詩云邦畿千里惟民所止。者詩商頌玄鳥之篇也邦畿王之都也止居也言物各有所當止之處也。詩云緡蠻黃鳥止于丘隅。子曰於止知其所止可以人而不如鳥乎。緡詩作縣蠻鳥聲○詩小雅緡蠻之篇緡蠻鳥聲丘隅岑蔚

大學

三　中華書局聚

之處人子當以知所當止孔子之說詩之

辭言人子當止於下引孔子之說詩之處也．詩云穆穆文王於緝熙

敬止爲人君止於仁爲人臣止於敬爲人子止於孝詩文王之篇穆穆．○

爲人父止於慈與國人交止於信詩緝王之篇音烏言其

深遠之意於歎美辭緝繼也熙光明也敬止無非至言至善其

無不敬而安所止也引此繼而言聖人之止無非至言

又五者乃其目之大者也學者於此究其精微之蘊而

疑推類以盡其餘則於天下之事皆有以知其所止而

而無詩云瞻彼淇澳菉竹猗猗有斐君子如切如磋

如琢如磨瑟兮僩兮赫兮喧兮有斐君子終不可諠

如切如磋者道學也如琢如磨者自脩也瑟兮僩

兮者恂慄也赫兮喧兮者威儀也有斐君子終不可

諠兮者道盛德至善民之不能忘也澳於六反．菉詩音

阿，烏何反。僩，下版反。喧，詩作咺，況晚反。恂，鄭氏讀。○詩衛風淇澳之篇。淇，水名。澳，隈也。猗猗，美盛貌。興也。斐，文貌。切以刀鋸，琢以椎鑿，皆裁物使其成形。磋以鑢鐋，磨以沙石，皆治物使其滑澤也。治骨角者，既切而復磋之。治玉石者，既琢而復磨之。皆言其治之有緒，而益致其精也。瑟，嚴密之貌。僩，武毅之貌。赫喧，宣著盛大之貌。諠，忘也。道，言也。學，謂講習討論之事。自脩者，省察克治之功。恂慄，戰懼也。威，可畏也。儀，可象也。引詩而釋之，以明明明德者之止於至善。道學自脩，言其所以得之之由。恂慄威儀，言其德容表裏之盛。卒乃指其實而歎美之也。

詩云，於戲前王不忘。君子賢其賢而親其親，小人樂其樂而利其利，此以沒世不忘也。

於戲音嗚呼，樂音洛，音樂君子。○詩周頌烈文之篇。於戲，歎辭。前王，謂文武也。君子，謂其後賢後王。小人，謂後民也。此言前王所以新民者止於至善，能使天下後世無一物不得其所，所以既沒世而人思慕之，愈久而不忘也。此兩節詠歎淫泆，其味深長，當熟玩之。

大學

四　中華書局聚

右傳之三章釋止於至善。此章內自引淇澳詩以下舊本誤在誠意章下。

子曰聽訟吾猶人也必也使無訟乎無情者不得盡其辭大畏民志此謂知本。引夫子之言而記之聖人能使無實以之畏人不敢盡其虛誕之辭蓋我之明德既明自然有以服民之心志故訟之不待聽而自無也。觀於此言之可以後知矣知本末之先後矣。

此謂知本。程子曰衍文也。

右傳之四章釋本末。此章舊本誤在止於信下。

此謂知之至也。此句之上別有闕文此特其結語耳。

右傳之五章蓋釋格物致知之義而今亡矣。此章舊本通下章。說在經文之下。

閒嘗竊取程子之意以補

VI.1

之曰所謂致知在格物者言欲致吾之知在
即物而窮其理也蓋人心之靈莫不有知而
天下之物莫不有理惟於理有未窮故其知
有不盡也是以大學始教必使學者即凡天
下之物莫不因其已知之理而益窮之以求
至乎其極至於用力之久而一旦豁然貫通
焉則衆物之表裏精粗無不到而吾心之全
體大用無不明矣此謂物格此謂知之至也

所謂誠其意者毋自欺也如惡惡臭如好好色此之
謂自謙故君子必慎其獨也

_{惡好上字皆去聲・謙讀}
_{爲慊苦劫反・○誠其意}

大學

五一中華書局聚

者自脩之首也。毋者。禁止之辭。自欺云者。知為善以去惡。而心之所發。有未實也。謙快也。足。快也。獨者。人所不知而己獨知之地也。言欲自脩者。知為善以去惡。則當實用其力。而禁止其自欺。使其惡惡則如惡惡臭。好善則如好好色。皆務決去而求必得之。以自快足於己。不可徒苟且以徇外而為人也。然其實與不實。蓋有他人所不及知。而己獨知之者。故必謹之於此以審其幾焉。

小人閒居為不善。無所不至。見君子而后厭然。揜其不善。而著其善。人之視己。如見其肺肝然。則何益矣。此謂誠於中形於外。故君子必慎其獨也。閒閒音閑。厭鄭氏讀為壓。○閒居。獨處也。厭然。消沮閉藏之貌。此言小人陰為不善。而陽欲揜之。則是非不知善之當為。與惡之當去也。但不能實用其力以至此耳。然則亦何益之有哉。此君子所以重以為戒。而必謹其獨也。

曾子曰。十目所視。十手所指。其嚴乎。上引此以明之意也。

大學

不可揜幽獨之中。而其善惡之甚也。○富潤屋德潤身心廣體

胖故君子必誠其意。能胖步丹反。德則能潤身矣言富故又言潤身此以結之也○胖安舒也言富則能潤屋矣德則能潤身矣故心無愧怍則廣大寬平而體常舒泰德之潤身者然也蓋善之實於中而形於外者如此故又言此以結之也

右傳之六章釋誠意。經曰欲誠其意先致其知。又曰知至而后意誠蓋心體之明有所未盡則其所發必有不能實用其力而苟焉以自欺者然既知為善以去其惡則當實用其力而禁止其自欺使其惡惡則如惡惡臭好善則如好好色皆務決去而求必得之以自快足於己不可徒苟且以徇外而為人也然其實與不實蓋有他人所不及知而己獨知之者故必謹之於此以審其幾焉

之謹乎此則其所明又非上章有以通考之然後進德之基故此則其所以明必誠承上章而言不可闕如此云序

右有以見其功用之始終如此云序

所謂脩身在正其心者身有所忿懥則不得其正有所恐懼則不得其正有所好樂則不得其正有所憂患則不得其正。懥敕值反好樂並去聲。○忿弗粉反。懥怒也。

身在正其心。

右傳之七章釋正心脩身。此章亦承上章以起下章。蓋意誠則真無惡而實有善矣。所以能存是心以檢其身。然或但知誠意而不能密察此心之存否則又無以直內而脩身也。故舊文齊正。○自此以下。並以舊文爲正。

所謂齊其家在脩其身者人之其所親愛而辟焉之其所賤惡而辟焉之其所畏敬而辟焉之其所哀矜而辟焉之其所敖惰而辟焉故好而知其惡惡而知

蓋是四者皆心之用而人所不能無者然一有之而不能察則欲動情勝而其用之所行或不能不失其正矣。

心不在焉視而不見聽而不聞食而不知其味。有心不存則無以檢其身是以君子必察乎此而敬以直之然後此心常存而身無不脩也。此謂脩身在正其心。

147

其美者，天下鮮矣。（鮮、辟，上聲。辟，讀為僻。○人謂衆人。之惡、敖、好、辟，並去聲。之，猶於也。辟，猶偏也。五者，在人本有當然之則；然常人之情，惟其所向而不加察焉，則必陷於一偏而身不脩矣。）故諺有之曰：「人莫知其子之惡，莫知其苗之碩。」此謂身不（諺，音彥。碩，葉韻。諺，俗語也。溺愛者不明，貪得者無厭，是則偏之為害，而家之所以不齊也。）脩不可以齊其家。

右傳之八章。釋脩身齊家。

所謂治國必先齊其家者，其家不可教而能教人者無之。故君子不出家而成教於國。孝者，所以事君也；弟者，所以事長也；慈者，所以使衆也。（○弟，去聲。○身脩，則家可教矣。孝弟慈所以脩身而教於家者也；然而國之所以事君、弟事長、使衆之道，不外乎此。此所以家齊於國之上……）

大學

七 十一 中華書局聚

IX.5　　　　　　　IX.4　　　IX.3　　IX.2

而教成也。康誥曰如保赤子心誠求之雖不中不遠矣

於下也。

未有學養子而后嫁者也。中去聲○此引書而釋之。又明立教之本不假強為。

在識其端而推廣之耳。

人貪戾一國作亂其機如此此謂一言僨事一人定

國。僨音奮○一人謂君也。機發動所由。僨覆敗也。此言教成於國之效。堯舜帥天下

一家仁一國興仁一家讓一國興讓一

以仁而民從之桀紂帥天下以暴而民從之其所令

反其所好而民不從是故君子有諸己而后求諸人。

無諸己而后非諸人所藏乎身不恕而能喻諸人者。

未之有也。惡去聲○此又承上文一人定國而言有善於己然後可以責人之善無惡於己然後

可以正人之惡皆推己以及人所謂恕也。不如是則所令反其所好。而民不從矣。喻曉也。故治

國在齊其家。〔上通文結。〕詩云桃之夭夭其葉蓁蓁之子于歸宜其家人宜其家人而后可以教國人。〔夭音夭平聲。○蓁詩真反。○詩周南桃夭之篇。夭夭，少好貌。蓁蓁，美盛貌。興也。之子，猶言是子也。此指女子之嫁者而言也。婦人謂嫁曰歸。宜猶善也。〕

詩云宜兄宜弟宜兄宜弟而后可以教國人。〔詩小雅蓼蕭篇。〕

詩云其儀不忒正是四國其為父子兄弟足法而后民法之也。〔詩曹風鳲鳩篇。忒，差也。〕

此謂治國在齊其家。〔詩皆以詠歎上文之事，而又結之如此。其味深長，最宜潛玩。〕

右傳之九章。釋齊家治國。

所謂平天下在治其國者上老老而民興孝上長長而民興弟上恤孤而民不倍是以君子有絜矩之道也

大學

八　中華書局聚

也。長、上聲。弟、去聲。倍、與背同。○老老，所謂老吾老也。興，謂有所感發而興起也。孤者，幼而無父之稱。絜，度也。矩，所以為方也。言此三者，上行下效，捷於影響，所謂家齊而國治也。亦可以見人心之所同，而不可使有一夫之不獲矣。是以君子必當因其所同，推以度物，使彼我之間，各得分願，則上下四旁，均齊方正，而天下平矣。

所惡於上，毋以使下；所惡於下，毋以事上；所惡於前，毋以先後；所惡於後，毋以從前；所惡於右，毋以交於左；所惡於左，毋以交於右。此之謂絜矩之道。○所惡、去聲。○此覆解上文絜矩二字之義。如不欲上之無禮於我，則必以此度下之心，而亦不敢以此無禮使之。不欲下之不忠於我，則必以此度上之心，而亦不敢以此不忠事之。至於前後左右，無不皆然，則身之所處，上下四旁，與長短廣狹，彼此如一，而無不方矣。彼同有是心而興起焉者，又豈有此一夫之不獲哉。所操者約，而所及者廣，此平天下之要道也。故章內之意，皆自此而推之。詩云：樂只君子，民之父母。民之所好好之，民之所惡惡之，此之謂民之父母。○樂音洛，只音紙，好惡並去聲。○詩小雅南山有臺之篇。只，語助辭。言能絜矩而以民心為己心，則是愛民如子，而民愛之如父母矣。

詩云，節彼南山，維石巖巖，赫赫師尹，民具爾瞻。有國者不可以不慎，辟則為天下僇矣。節讀為截，辟讀為僻，與戮同。○詩小雅節南山之篇。節，截然高大貌。師尹，周太師尹氏也。具，俱也。辟，偏也。言在上者人所瞻仰，不可不慎。若不能絜矩而好惡徇於一己者之偏，則身弒國亡，為天下之大僇矣。

詩云，殷之未喪師，克配上帝，儀監于殷，峻命不易。道得眾則得國，失眾則失國。喪去聲，儀詩作宜，峻詩作駿，易去聲。○詩文王篇。師，眾也。監，視也。配，對也。峻，大也。配上帝，不易，言難保者也。道，言此也。引詩而言此，以結上文兩節之意。有天下者能存此心而不失，則所以絜矩而與民同意。

大學

九 中華書局聚

152

X.12　X.11　　　　X.10　X.9　X.8　X.7　　　X.6

能已矣。

是故君子先慎乎德。有德此有人。有人此有土。有土此有財。有財此有用。
先慎乎德而言。承上文。不慎所
謂明德。有人則謂得眾。有土則謂得國。有財則不患無財。有用矣。

德者本也。財者末也。本上

外本內末。爭民施奪。
人君以德為外。以財為內。則是爭鬥其民。而施之以劫奪之教也。蓋財者人之所同欲。不能絜矩而欲專之。則民亦起而爭奪矣。

是故財聚則民散。財散則民聚。
外本內末。故財聚。爭民施奪。故有財聚。而有民矣。是

故言悖而出者。亦悖而入。貨悖而入者。亦悖而出。
悖布。悖逆也。此以言之出入。明貨之出入也。又因財貨之出入。以明能絜矩與不能者先。自先慎乎德以下至此。

康誥曰。惟命不于常。道善則得之。不善則失之矣。
慎乎德。以下至此。又因財貨以明能絜矩與不能者之得失也。

矣。楚書曰。楚國
失之也。得之道言也。因上文引文王詩之意。而申其丁寧反覆之意益深切矣。言其地。

無以爲寶惟善以爲寶。〔鍰書鍰語言人不寶金玉而寶善人也。〕舅犯曰亡

人無以爲寶仁親以爲寶。〔舅犯晉文公舅狐偃字子犯也亡人文公時爲公子〕

斷斷兮無他技其心休休焉其如有容焉人之有技〔秦誓周書若有一个臣〕

若己有之人之彥聖其心好之不啻若自其口出寔

能容之以能保我子孫黎民尚亦有利哉人之有技

媢疾以惡之人之彥聖而違之俾不通寔不能容以

不能保我子孫黎民亦曰殆哉〔殆丁代反書作介亂反書媢音冒。○斷〕

唯仁人放

流之迸諸四夷不與同中國此謂唯仁人爲能愛人

〔兩節又明不外本而內末之意。亡在外也。仁愛也。事見檀弓之意〕

〔斷斷誠一之貌。彥美士也。聖通明也。尚庶幾也。媢忌也。違拂戾也。殆危也。〕

欲者省。
已矣。

是故君子先慎乎德。有德此有人，有人此

有土，有土此有財，有財此有用。德者本也，財者末也。 上本
得謂明德。有人則不患眾無財有用矣。謂 可不慎乎德承上文而言。德即所
訖。外本內末，爭民施奪。 則人之所同欲不能
劫奪之教也。蓋財者人亦起而爭奪矣。 是故財聚則
民散，財散則民聚。 民外本反是則有德聚而有人矣。故
故言悖而出者，亦悖而入；貨悖而入者，亦悖而出。 悖布
慎內叛德。○悖逆也。此又因財貨以明能絜矩與不能者先
失之得也。康誥曰：惟命不于常，道善則得之，不善則失之
矣。謂之言其地。因上文覆之意益深切而申。楚書曰楚國

珍做宋版却

153

無以為寶，惟善以為寶。檀弓、楚書、楚語，言人不寶金玉而寶善人也。舅犯曰：亡人無以為寶，仁親以為寶。舅犯，狐偃字子犯，晉文公時為公子，出亡在外也。仁，愛也。事見檀弓。此兩節又明不外本而内末之意。此

秦誓曰：若有一个臣，斷斷今無他技，其心休休焉，其如有容焉。人之有技，若己有之；人之彥聖，其心好之，不啻若自其口出，寔能容之，以能保我子孫黎民，尚亦有利哉！人之有技，媢疾以惡之；人之彥聖，而違之俾不通，寔不能容，以不能保我子孫黎民，亦曰殆哉！个，古賀反。○迸，書作屏，必郢反。媢，音冒。○秦誓，周書。斷斷，誠一之貌。彥，美士也。聖，通明也。尚，庶幾也。媢，忌也。違，拂戾也。殆，危也。唯仁人放流之，迸諸四夷，不與同中國，此謂唯仁人為能愛人。

大學

十

中華書局聚

能惡人。迸讀爲屏古字通用。○迸猶逐也。言有此媚疾之人妨賢而病國則仁人必深惡而痛絕之。

得之以好惡其之至公如此無私也。故能見賢而不能舉舉而不能先。

命也見不善而不能退退而不能遠過也。當命作慢○程氏云

惡子．云當作怠未能盡愛惡之是遠去聲○若而惡未仁者如所愛好

人之所惡惡人之所好是謂拂人之性菑必逮夫身。

至菑从災古字夫人字之音扶．○拂逆之甚者也．好善而惡惡者也．自而惡惡人之性也．此又皆

文以申言好惡南山有臺節南山之明上意是故君子有大道必

忠信以得之驕泰以失之位君子以位言之倚己治人之道謂居其

上所盡爲忠循物無違之意謂信章內孫三言得失而肆此因

理如切亡蓋至此而天生財有大道生之者眾食之者寡

爲之者疾。用之者舒。則財恆足矣。恆胡登反。呂氏曰。國無遊民。則生者衆矣。朝無幸位。則食之者寡矣。不奪農時。則爲之者疾矣。量入爲出。則用之者舒矣。愚按此因有土有財而言。以明足國之道。在乎務本而節用。非必外本內末而後財可聚也。自此以至終篇。皆一意也。

仁者以財發身。不仁者以身發財。發猶起也。仁者散財以得民。不仁者亡身以殖貨。

未有上好仁而下不好義者也。未有好義其事不終者也。未有府庫財非其財者也。則上好仁以愛其下。下好義以忠其上。所以事必有終。而府庫之財無悖出之患也。

孟獻子曰。畜馬乘不察於雞豚。伐冰之家不畜牛羊。百乘之家不畜聚斂之臣。與其有聚斂之臣。寧有盜臣。此謂國不以利爲利。以義爲利也。畜許六反。乘去聲。斂去聲。○孟獻子魯之賢大夫仲孫蔑也。畜馬乘士初試爲大夫者也。伐

大學

冰之家。卿大夫以上喪祭用冰者也。百乘之家有采地者也。君子寧以己之財而不忍傷民之力。故寧有盜臣而不畜聚斂之臣。此謂以下而不釋獻于聚斂之訓也。此釋長國家而務財用者必自小人矣。彼為善之小人之使為國家菑害並至雖有善者亦無如之何矣。此謂國不以利為利以義為利也。長上言由小人導之此句上下疑有闕文誤字○自利之由上聲彼為善之善以利為利之自利之自此一節深明以利為利之害而重言以結之。其丁寧之意以如此矣。

右傳之十章釋治國平天下。此與民章之義務在好惡而不專其利。皆推廣其絜矩之意。下也能如是則親賢樂利各得其所矣。凡傳

十章前四章統論綱領指趣。後六章細論條

目工夫其第五章乃明善之要第六章乃誠

身之本在初學尤爲當務之急讀者不可以

其近而忽之也

大學

十二 中華書局聚

記大學後

右大學一篇經二百有五字傳十章今見於戴氏禮書而

簡編散脫傳文頗失其次子程子蓋嘗正之熹不自揆竊

因其說復定此本蓋傳之一章釋明明德二章釋新民三

章釋止於至善以上並從程本而增詩云瞻彼其澳以下四章釋本末五章釋

致知並今六章釋誠意本從程本

身齊家九章釋齊家治國平天下舊本頗有錯簡今因七章釋正心脩身八章釋脩

貫似得其真謹第錄如上其先賢所正衍文誤字皆存其

本文而圍其上旁注所改又與今所疑者并見於釋音云

新安朱熹謹記

BIBLIOGRAPHY GLOSSARY INDEX

Bibliography

The following abbreviations are used in the list of works cited:

HYISIS Harvard-Yenching Institute Sinological Index Series. Pei-p'ing: Yen-ching University, 1931-1947.

SSCCS *Shih-san ching chu-shu* 十三經注疏. Compiled by Juan Yuan 阮 元 (1764-1849). Taipei: I-wen yin-shu kuan, 1965 (photographic reproduction of 1815, Nan-ch'ang edition).

Abei Bōzan 安部井帽山. *Shisho kummō shūso* 四書訓蒙輯疏 1848 edition.
Akatsuka Kiyoshi 赤塚忠. *Daigaku Chūyō* 大學中庸. Vol. II of *Shinshaku Kambun taikei* 新釈漢文大系. Tokyo, Meiji shoin, 1967.

Biot, Edouard. *Le Tcheou-li, ou Rites des Tcheou.* 2 vols. Paris, Imprimerie nationale, 1851.

Chai Hao 翟灝. *Ssu-shu k'ao-i* 四書考異. 1769 edition.
Chan, Hok-lam and Wm. Theodore de Bary, eds. *Yüan Thought: Chinese Thought and Religion Under the Mongols.* New York, Columbia University Press, 1982.
Chan, Wing-tsit. "Chu Hsi's Completion of Neo-Confucianism," in *Etudes Song: In Memoriam Etienne Balazs.* Ed. Francoise Aubin. Series II, no. 1 (1973).
———. "The Evolution of the Neo-Confucian Concept *Li* as Principle," in *Neo-Confucianism, Etc.: Essays by Wing-Tsit Chan.* Comp. Charles K. H. Chen. Hanover, Oriental Society, 1969.
———. *Reflections on Things at Hand.* New York, Columbia University Press, 1967.
———. *A Source Book in Chinese Philosophy.* Princeton, Princeton University Press, 1963.
———. "The Study of Chi Hsi in the West," *Journal of Asian Studies* 35.4:555-577 (August 1976).
———. "Wang Yang-ming: Western Studies and an Annotated Bibliography," *Philosophy East and West* 22:75-92 (1972).
Chang Tsai 張載. *Chang-tzu ch'üan-shu* 張子全書. *Kuo-hsueh chi-pen ts'ung shu* 國學基本叢書 edition.
Chao Tse-hou 趙澤厚. *Ta-hsueh yen-chiu* 大學研究. Taipei, Chung-hua shu-chü, 1962.

BIBLIOGRAPHY

Chavannes. Edouard. *Les Mémoires historiques de Se-ma Ts'ien.* 5 vols. Paris, Leroux, 1895–1905.

Ch'en Chen-sun 陳振孫. *Chih-chai shu-lu chieh t'i* 直齋書錄解題 *Ts'ung-shu chi-ch'eng* 叢書集成 edition.

Ch'en Ti 陳第. *Shih-shan t'ang tsang-shu mu-lu* 世善堂藏書目錄. *Ts'ung-shu chi-ch'eng* edition.

Ch'eng Hao 程顥 and Ch'eng I 程頤. *Ho-nan Ch'eng-shih ching-shuo* 河南程氏經說. In *Erh-Ch'eng ch'üan-shu* 二程全書 *Ssu-pu pei-yao* 四部備要 edition.

————. *Ho-nan Ch'eng-shih i-shu* 河南程氏遺書. *Kuo-hsueh chi-pen ts'ung-shu* edition.

————. *Ho-nan Ch'eng-shih wai-shu* 河南程氏外書. In *Erh-Ch'eng ch'üan-shu. Ssu-pu pei-yao* edition.

Ch'eng I. *I-ch'uan hsien-sheng wen-chi* 伊川先生文集. In *Erh-Ch'eng ch'üan-shu. Ssu-pu pei-yao* edition.

————. *I-ch'uan I-ch'uan* 伊川易傳, in *Erh-Ch'eng ch'üan-shu. Ssu-pu pei-yao* edition.

Ch'ien Mu 錢穆. *Chu-tzu hsin hsueh-an* 朱子新學案. 5 vols. Taipei, San-min shu-chü, 1971.

————. *Chung-kuo chin san-pai nien hsueh-shu shih* 中國近三百年學術史. 2 vols. Taipei, Commercial Press, 1957.

————. "Ssu-pu kai-lun" 四部概論. In *Chung-kuo hsueh-shu t'ung-i* 中國學術通義. Taipei, Hsueh-sheng shu-chü, 1975.

Chiu T'ang shu 舊唐書. Peking, Chung-hua shu-chü, 1975.

Chou i 周易. HYISIS, Supplement no. 10.

Chou li 周禮. SSCCS edition.

Chu Hsi 朱熹. *Chu-tzu yü-lei* 朱子語類. Ed. Li Ching-te 黎靖德 1880 edition.

————. *Hui-an hsien-sheng Chu Wen-kung hsü-chi* 晦庵先生朱文公續集. *Ssu-pu ts'ung-k'an* edition.

————. *Hui-an hsien-sheng Chu Wen-kung wen-chi* 晦庵先生朱文公文集. *Ssu-pu ts'ung-k'an* edition.

————. *Hui-an hsien-sheng Chu Wen-kung pieh-chi* 晦庵先生朱文公別集. *Ssu-pu ts'ung-k'an* edition.

————. *Lun-yü chi-chu* 論語集注. In *Ssu-shu chi-chu* 四書集注. *Ssu-pu pei-yao* edition.

————. *Ta-hsueh chang-chü* 大學章句. In *Ssu-shu chi-chu. Ssu-pu pei yao* edition.

————. *Ta-hsueh huo-wen* 大學或問. In *Ssu-shu ta-ch'üan* 四書大全 Japanese edition of 1626 based on *Yung-lo* edition of 1415.

Chu I-tsun 朱彝尊. *Ching-i k'ao* 經義考. *Ssu-pu pei-yao* edition.

Ch'ü Wan-li 屈萬里. "Sung-jen i ching te feng-ch'i" 宋人疑經的風氣, *Ta-lu tsa-chih* 大陸雜誌. 29.3:23–25 (August 1964).

Ch'un-ch'iu 春秋. HYISIS, Supplement no. 11.

Chung-yung 中庸. References are to standard chapter and verse numbers.

de Bary, Wm. Theodore. *The Liberal Tradition in China*. Hong Kong, Chinese University Press, 1983.

———. *Neo-Confucian Orthodoxy and the Learning of the Mind-and-Heart*. New York, Columbia University Press, 1981.

de Bary, Wm. Theodore and Irene Bloom, eds. *Principle and Practicality: Essays in Neo-Confucianism and Practical Learning*. New York, Columbia University Press, 1979.

———. "A Reappraisal of Neo-Confucianism," in *Studies in Chinese Thought*. Ed. Arthur Wright. Chicago, University of Chicago Press, 1953.

———, ed. *Sources of Chinese Tradition*, Vol. I. New York, Columbia University Press, 1960.

Dubs, Homer. *History of the Former Han Dynasty*. 3 vols. Baltimore, Waverly Press, Inc., 1938.

Fumoto Yasutaka 麓保孝 . "Daigaku o chūshin to shitaru Sōdai jugaku" 大學を中心としたる宋代儒學 , *Shingaku kenkyū* 支那學研究 3:269-309 (1949).

Fung Yu-lan. *A History of Chinese Philosophy*, 2 vols. Tr. Derk Bodde. Princeton, Princeton University Press, 1953.

Fung Yu-lan 馮友蘭 . "Ta-hsueh wei Hsun-hsueh shuo" 大學為荀學說 , *Yen-ching hsueh-pao* 燕京學報 7:1319-1326 (1930).

Gardner, Daniel K. "Chu Hsi's Reading of the *Ta-hsüeh*: A Neo-Confucian's Quest for Truth." *Journal of Chinese Philosophy* 10.3:183-204 (September 1983).

———. "Principle and Pedagogy: Chu Hsi and the Four Books," *Harvard Journal of Asiatic Studies* 44.1:57-81 (June 1984).

———. "Transmitting the Way: Chu Hsi and His Program of Learning." Forthcoming in a volume ed. Wm. Theodore de Bary, consisting of essays originally prepared for the conference Neo-Confucian Education: The Formative State, Princeton, September 1984.

Giles, Herbert A. *A Chinese Biographical Dictionary*. Reprint. Taipei, Ch'eng-wen Publishing Co., 1971.

Graham, A. C. *Two Chinese Philosophers: Ch'eng Ming-Tao and Ch'eng Yi-ch'uan*. London, Lund Humphries, 1958.

Han shu 漢書 . Peking, Chung-hua shu-chü, 1962.

Han Yü 韓愈 . *Chu Wen-kung chiao Ch'ang-li hsien-sheng wen-chi* 朱文公校昌黎先生文集 . *Ssu-pu ts'ung-k'an* edition.

Honda Nariyuki 本田成之 . *Shina keigaku shiron* 支那經學史論 . Tr. Chiang Hsia-an 江俠菴 . *Ching-hsueh shih-lun* 經學史論 Shanghai, Commercial Press, 1934.

Hsu Fu-kuan 徐復觀 . *Chung-kuo jen-hsing lun shih* 中國人性論史 T'aichung, Chung-yang shu-chü, 1963.

Hsun-tzu chi-chieh 荀子集解 . Edited by Wang Hsien-chien 王先謙 1891 edition.

Hu Shih. "The Establishment of Confucianism as a State Religion During the Han Dynasty," *Journal of the North China Branch of the Royal Asiatic Society* 60:20–41 (1929).

Huan K'uan 桓寬 . *Yen-t'ieh lun* 鹽鐵論 . *Ssu-pu ts'ung-k'an* edition.

Ichikawa Yasuji 市川安司 . "Shushi gorui zakki" 朱子語類雜記 *Jimbun kagakuka kiyō* 人文科學科紀要 21:137–184 (1959).

———. *Tei I-sen tetsugaku no kenkyū* 程伊川哲學の研究 . Tokyo, Tokyo University Press, 1964.

Kano Naoki 狩野直喜 *Chūgoku tetsugaku shi* 中國哲學史 . Tokyo, Iwanami shoten, 1953.

Kao Ch'eng 高承 . *Shih-wu chi-yuan chi-lei* 事物紀原集類 . Facsimile reproduction of 1447 edition. Taipei, Hsin-hsing shu-chü, 1969.

Kao Ming 高明 . "Ta-hsueh pien" 大學辨 , in *Li-hsueh hsin-t'an* 禮學新探 . Hong Kong, Lien-ho shu-yuan, 1963.

Karlgren, Bernhard. *The Book of Documents*. Reprinted from the *Bulletin of the Museum of Far Eastern Antiquities,* 22:1–81 (1950).

———. *The Book of Odes*. Stockholm, The Museum of Far Eastern Antiquities, 1950.

———. "Glosses on the *Book of Documents,*" *Bulletin of the Museum of Far Eastern Antiquities* 20:39–312 (1948).

Ku-liang chuan 穀梁傳 (in *Ch'un-ch'iu ching-chuan yin-te* 春秋經傳引得). HYISIS, Supplement no. 11.

Kung-yang chuan 公羊傳 . SSCCS edition.

Kuo-yü 國語 . *Ssu-pu ts'ung-k'an* edition.

Kusumoto Bun'yū 久須本雄 . *Sōdai Jugaku no Zen shisō kenkyū* 宋代儒學の禪思想研究 . Nagoya, Nisshindō shoten, 1980.

D. C. Lau. *The Analects*. Harmondsworth, Penguin, 1979.

———. *Mencius*. Harmondsworth, Penguin, 1970.

———. "A Note on Ke Wu 格物 ," *Bulletin of the School of Oriental and African Studies,* 30:353–357 (1967).

Legge, James. *The Chinese Classics*. 5 vols. Rev. edition. Hong Kong, Hong Kong University Press, 1960.

———. *Li Ki*. 2 vols. Vols. 27 and 28 of the *Sacred Books of the East*. Ed. F. Max Müller. Oxford, Clarendon Press, 1885.

Li Ao 李翱 . *Li Wen-kung chi* 李文公集 . *Ssu-pu ts'ung-k'an* edition.

Li chi 禮記 . SSCCS edition.

Li T'ao 李燾 . *Hsu Tzu-chih t'ung-chien ch'ang-pien* 續資治通鑑長編 . Taipei, Shih-chieh shu-chü, 1974.

Liu Chih-chi 劉知幾 . *Shih t'ung* 史通 . *Ssu-pu ts'ung-k'an* edition.

Liu, James T. C. "An Early Sung Reformer: Fan Chung-yen," in *Chinese Thought and Institutions*. Ed. John K. Fairbank. Chicago, University of Chicago Press, 1957.

———. *Ou-yang Hsiu: An Eleventh-Century Neo-Confucianist*. Stanford, Stanford University Press, 1967.

———. *Reform in Sung China: Wang An-shih (1021–1086) and His New Policies*. Cambridge, Harvard University Press, 1959.

Lu Ch'un 陸淳 . *Ch'un-ch'iu chi-chuan tsuan-li* 春秋集傳纂例 *Ku ching chieh hui han edition*, 1873.

Lun-yü 論語 . HYISIS, Supplement no. 16.

Ma Tsung-huo 馬宗霍 . *Chung-kuo ching-hsueh shih* 中國經學史 . Taipei, Commercial Press, 1972.

Mathews' Chinese-English Dictionary. Revised American edition. Cambridge, Harvard University Press, 1960.

Meng-tzu 孟子 . HYISIS, Supplement no. 17.

Metzger, Thomas. *Escape from Predicament: Neo-Confucianism and China's Evolving Political Culture*. New York, Columbia University Press, 1977.

Morohashi Tetsuji 諸橋轍次 . *Daigaku Chūyō* 大學中庸 . Vol. V of *Kambun kōza* 漢文講座 . Tokyo, Kōdōkan, 1931.

———. *Dai kanwa jiten* 大漢和辭典 . 13 vols. Tokyo, Daishūkan shoten, 1955–1960.

———. *Jugaku no mokuteki to Sō-ju no katsudō* 儒學の目的と宋儒の活動 . Vol. I of *Morohashi Tetsuji chosaku shū* 諸橋轍次著作集 . Tokyo, Daishūkan shoten, 1936.

———. *Keigaku kenkyū josetsu* 經學研究序說 . Tokyo, Meguro shoten, 1975.

Nagasawa Kikuya 長澤規矩也 . *Shina gakujutsu bungeishi* 支那學術文藝史 . Tokyo, Sanseidō, 1938.

Nivison, David. "Introduction," in *Confucianism in Action*. Ed. David Nivison and Arthur Wright. Stanford, Stanford University Press, 1959.

Ou-yang Hsiu 歐陽修 . *Ou-yang Wen-chung-kung chi* 歐陽文忠公集 . *Ssu-pu ts'ung-k'an* edition.

P'i Hsi-jui 皮錫瑞 . *Ching-hsueh li-shih* 經學歷史 . Taipei, Ho-lo tu-shu ch'u-pan she, 1974.

Po-hu t'ung 白虎通 (*Po-hu t'ung te lun* 白虎通德論). *Ssu-pu ts'ung-k'an* edition.

Po Shou-i 白壽彝 . *Ts-ung-cheng chi chiang-hsueh chung-te Chu Hsi* 從政及講座中的朱熹 . Peking, Kuo-li Pei-p'ing yen-chiu yuan, 1931.

Pulleyblank, E.G. "Chinese Historical Criticism: Liu Chih-chi and Ssu-ma Kuang," in *Historians of China and Japan*. Ed. W.G. Beasley and E.G. Pulleyblank. London, Oxford University Press, 1961.

———. "Neo-Confucianism and Neo-Legalism in T'ang Intellectual Life, 755–805," in *The Confucian Persuasion*. Ed. Arthur Wright. Stanford, Stanford University Press, 1960.

Sargent, Galen. *Tchou Hi contre le Bouddhisme*. Paris, Imprimerie nationale, 1955.

Schirokauer, Conrad M. "Chu Hsi's Political Career: A Study in Ambivalence." In *Confucian Personalities*. Ed. Arthur Wright and Denis Twitchett. Stanford, Stanford University Press, 1962.

Schwartz, Benjamin I. "Some Polarities in Confucian Thought," in *Confucianism in Action*. Ed. David Nivison and Arthur Wright. Stanford, Stanford University Press, 1959.

Shang shu 尚書 . SSCCS edition.

Shih ching 詩經 . References are to standard Mao ode and verse numbers.

Shimada Kenji 島田虔次 . *Daigaku Chūyō* 大學中庸 . Vol. IV of *Chū-goku kotensen* 中國古典選 . Tokyo, Asahi shimbunsha, 1967.

———. *Shushigaku to Yōmeigaku* 朱子學と陽明學 . Tokyo, Iwanami shoten, 1967.

Shryock, John K. *The Origin and Development of the State Cult of Confucius*. New York, Paragon Book Reprint Corp., 1966.

Soothill, William Edward. *A Dictionary of Chinese Buddhist Terms*. 1937 edition; reprint. Kaohsiung, Buddhist Culture Service, 1971.

Ssu-k'u ch'üan-shu tsung-mu t'i-yao 四庫全書總目提要 . 5 vols. Taipei, Commercial Press, 1971.

Ssu-ma Ch'ien 司馬遷 . *Shih chi* 史記 . *Shiki kaichū kōshō* 史記會注考證 edition. Compiled and annotated by Takigawa Kametarō 龍川龜太郎 . 10 vols. Tokyo, Tōhō bunka gakuin, 1932–1934.

Ssu-ma Kuang 司馬光 . *Wen-kuo Wen-cheng Ssu-ma kung wen-chi* 溫國文正司馬公文集 . *Ssu-pu ts'ung-k'an* edition.

Ssu-shu ta-ch'üan 四書大全 . Japanese edition of 1626 based on *Yung-lo* edition of 1415.

Su Shih 蘇軾 . *T'ung-p'o hsien-sheng shu chuan* 東坡先生書傳 . In *Liang-Su ching-chieh*. 1597 edition.

Sung hui-yao chi-kao 宋會要輯稿. Recollected from the *Yung-lo ta-tien* 永樂大典 in 1809–1810 by Hsu Sung 徐松 . Peking, Chung-hua shu-chü, 1957.

Sung-jen chuan-chi tzu-liao so-yin 宋人傳記資料索引 . Comp. Ch'ang Pi-te 昌彼得 , Ch'eng Yuan-min 程元敏 , and Wang Te-i 王德毅 . 6 vols. Taipei, Ting-wen shu-chü, 1974–1976.

Sung shih 宋史 . *Po-na* edition.

Sung, Z. D. *The Text of Yi King: Chinese Original with English Translation*. Shanghai, The Modern China Education Co., 1935.

Ta-hsüeh tsuan-shu 大學纂疏 . In *Ssu-shu tsuan-shu* 四書纂疏. Ed. Chao Shun-sun 趙順孫 . Reprint of *T'ung-chih t'ang* 通志堂 edition. Kaohsiung. Ch'i-sheng t'u-shu kung-ssu, 1973.

Tai Chün-jen 戴君仁 . "Hsun-tzu yü *Ta-hsueh Chung-yung*" 荀子與大學中庸 , *K'ung-Meng hsueh-pao* 孔孟學報 15:91–103 (1968).

Takeuchi Yoshio 武內義雄 . *Chūgoku shisō shi* 中國思想史 . Tokyo, Iwanami shoten, 1936.

———. "Daigakuhen seritsu nendai kō" 大學篇成立年代攷 , in *Rōshi genshi* 老子原始 . Tokyo, Shimizu kōbundō shobō, 1967.

T'ang Chün-i 唐君毅 . "Ta-hsueh chang-chü pien-cheng chi ko wu chih chih ssu-hsiang chih fa-chan" 大學章句辯證及格物致知思想之發展 , *Ch'ing-hua hsueh-pao* 清華學報 , New Series 4.2:1–49 (February 1964).

Teng, Ssu-yü and Knight Biggerstaff. *An Annotated Bibliography of Selected Chinese Reference Works*. Third edition. Cambridge, Harvard University Press, 1971.

Tillman, Hoyt C. *Utilitarian Confucianism: Ch'en Liang's Challenge to Chu Hsi*. Cambridge, The Council on East Asian Studies, Harvard University, 1982.

Tjan Tjoe Som. *Po Hu T'ung: The Comprehensive Discussions in the White Tiger Hall.* 2 vols. Leiden, Brill, 1949.

Toda Toyosaburō 戸田豐三郎 . "Sōdai ni okeru Daigakuhen hyōshō no shimatsu 宋代におけ る 大學篇表章の始末 , Tōhōgaku 東方學 21:46–56 (1961).

Ts'ai Hsu-chai 蔡虛齋 . *Ssu-shu meng-yin* 四書蒙引 . Vol. CX of *Ssu-ku ch'üan-shu chen-pen* 四庫全書珍本 , 3rd Series. Taipei, Commercial Press, 1972.

Ts'ai Jen-hou 蔡仁厚 . "Ta-hsueh fen-chang chih yen-chiu" 大學分章之 研究 , *K'ung-Meng hsueh-pao* 孔孟學報, 9:53–76 (1965).

Ts'ai Yung-ch'un. *The Philosophy of Ch'eng I: A Selection of Texts from the Complete Works. Edited and Translated with Introduction and Notes.* Ann Arbor, University Microfilms International, 1950.

Tso chuan 左傳 . HYISIS, Supplement no. 11.

Tu, Wei-ming. "The Great Learning in Neo-Confucian Thought." Paper presented at the Annual Meeting of the Association for Asian Studies. Toronto, 19 March 1976.

———. "Reconstituting the Confucian Tradition." (Review of Ch'ien Mu's *Chu-tzu hsin hsueh-an*). *The Journal of Asian Studies* 33.3:441–454 (May 1974).

Waley, Arthur. *The Analects of Confucius.* New York, Vintage, 1938.

Wallacker, Benjamin E. "Han Confucianism and Confucius in Han," in *Ancient China: Studies in Early Civilization.* Ed. David T. Roy and Tsuen-hsuin Tsien. Hong Kong, The Chinese University Press, 1978.

Wang Kuo-wei 王國維 . "Han-Wei po-shih k'ao" 漢魏博士考 . *Wang Kuan-t'ang hsien-sheng ch'üan-chi* 王觀堂先生全集 , Vol. 1. Taipei, Wen-hua ch'u-pan kung-ssu, 1968.

Wang Mou-hung 王懋竑. *Chu-tzu nien-p'u* 朱子年譜 . *Ts'ung-shu chi-ch'eng* edition.

Wang Ying-lin 王應麟. *K'un-hsueh chi-wen* 困學紀問 . *Ssu-pu ts'ung k'an* edition.

———. *Yü-hai* 玉海 . Chekiang shu-chü, 1883.

Watson, Burton, tr. *Records of the Grand Historian of China.* 2 vols. New York, Columbia University Press, 1961.

———. *Ssu-ma Ch'ien: Grand Historian of China.* New York, Columbia University Press, 1958.

Wei Po-yang 魏伯陽 . *Ts'an-t'ung-ch'i cheng-wen* 參同契正文 . *Ts'ung-shu chi-ch'eng* edition.

Yamashita Ryūji 山下龍二 . *Daigaku Chūyō* 大學中庸 . Vol. III of *Zensaku kambun taikei* 全釈漢文大系 . Tokyo, Shūeisha, 1974.

Yang Hsiung 揚雄 . *Yang-tzu fa-yen* 揚子法言 . *Ssu-pu ts'ung-k'an* edition.

Yü Ying-shih. "Some Preliminary Observations on the Rise of Ch'ing Confucian Intellectualism," *Tsing Hua Journal of Chinese Studies,* New Series 11.1 and 2:105–146 (December 1975).

Yuan shih 元史 . Peking, Chung-hua shu-chü, 1976.

Glossary

This list excludes common place-names and most of the names and titles in the Bibliography.

Chai Hao 翟灝
Chang-chou 漳州
Chang I 張儀
Chang Nan-hsien 張南軒
Chang Tsai 張載
Chao K'uang 趙匡
Ch'en Ch'un 陳淳
Cheng Hsuan 鄭玄
Cheng-meng 正蒙
Ch'eng Hao 程顥
Ch'eng I 程頤
Ch'eng-i lang 承議郎
Chi Ta-hsueh hou 記大學後
ch'i 氣
Ch'ien Mu 錢穆
chih 至
chih ch'i-chih 致其知
chih chih 致知
chih chih tsai ko wu 致知在格物
chih chih tsai ko wu lun 致知在格物論
chin-shih 進士
Chin-ssu lu 近思錄

ching 敬
ching 經
ch'ing 情
ch'iung li 窮理
Ch'iung lin 瓊林
Chou i ts'an-t'ung ch'i k'ao i 周易參同契考異
Chou i t'ung-tzu-wen 周易童子問
Chou li 周禮
Chou li hsin-i 周禮新義
Chou Tun-i 周敦頤
Chu Hsi 朱熹
Chu Sung 朱松
Chu-tzu nien-p'u 朱子年譜
Chu-tzu yü-lei 朱子語類
chü ching 居敬
Ch'u yü 楚語
Ch'ü-li 曲禮
chuan 傳
chüan 卷
Ch'un-ch'iu 春秋
Chung-sun Mieh 仲孫蔑
Chung-yung 中庸

Chung-yung chang-chü 中庸章句
Chung-yung Ta-hsueh kuang-i
　　中庸大學廣義
Ch'ung-cheng-tien shuo-shu
　　崇政殿説書

Erh-ya 爾雅

Fan Chung-yen 范仲淹
Fan Tsu-yü 范祖禹
feng-shih 封事
Fu-hsing shu 復性書

han 扞
Han Fei 韓非
Han Yü 韓愈
Ho-nan Ch'eng-shih ching-shuo
　　河南程氏經説
Ho-nan Ch'eng-shih i-shu
　　河南程氏遺書
Ho-nan Ch'eng-shih wai-shu
　　河南程氏外書
Hsi-tz'u 繫辭
Hsiang-shuo 詳説
Hsiao ching 孝經
hsiao-tzu chih hsueh 小子之學
Hsieh Shang-ts'ai 謝上蔡
hsin min 新民
hsing 性
hsing-ch'i chih ssu 形氣之私
Hsiung An-sheng 熊安生
hsu 虛
Hsu Shun-chih 許順之
Hu An-kuo 胡安國

Hu Ping-wen 胡炳文
Hu Yen 狐偃 (*tzu* Tzu Fan 子犯)
Hu Yuan 胡瑗
Huang-chi ching-shih 皇極經世
Huang Kan 黄榦
Huang K'an 皇侃
Hui-an hsien-sheng Chu Wen-kung
　　wen-chi 晦庵先生朱文公
　　　文集
Huo-wen 或問

I ching 易經
I-ch'uan hsien-sheng kai-cheng Ta-
　　hsueh 伊川先生改正大學
I-ch'uan I chuan 伊川易傳
I-ch'uan I chuan hsu 伊川易傳序
I li 儀禮
I shuo 易説

jen-hsin 人心
Ju-hsing 儒行
Ju-hsueh chuan 儒學傳
Ju-lin chuan 儒林傳

kang-ling 網領
k'ao-cheng 考證
ko 格
ko wu 格物
Ku-liang chuan 穀梁傳
Ku ming 顧命
ku-wen 古文
Kuan She-fu 觀射父
Kuan-tzu 管子

Kung-sun Hung 公孫弘
Kung-yang 公羊
Kung-yang chuan 公羊傳
K'ung An-kuo 孔安國
K'ung-shih i-shu 孔氏遺書
K'ung Ying-ta 孔穎達
Kuo yü 國語
Kuo Yu-jen 郭友仁

lai 來
li 理
Li Ao 李翱
Li chi 禮記
Li chi cheng-i 禮記正義
Li chi chu 禮記注
Li Wen-ching 李文靖
Lin Tse-chih 李擇之
ling 靈
Liu Ch'ang 劉敞
Liu Chih-chi 劉知幾
Liu Ch'ing-chih 劉清之
Lu Yu 陸游
Lü Kung-chu 呂公著
Lü Ta-lin 呂大臨
Lü Tsu-ch'ien 呂祖謙
Lun-yü 論語

Meng-tzu 孟子
Ming-tao hsien-sheng hsing-chuang 明道先生行狀
Ming-tao hsien-sheng kai-cheng Ta-hsueh 明道先生改正大學
ming-te 明德
Mo Ti 墨翟

Nei-tse 內則
Ou-yang Hsiu 歐陽修
P'an Tuan-shu 潘端叔
pu-chuan 補傳
Shang Yang 商鞅
Shao-i 少儀
Shao Yung 邵雍
Shen Pu-hai 申不害
Sheng-jen chih wan-shu 聖人之完書
shih 事
Shih chi 史記
Shih ching 詩經
Shih-ch'ü 石渠
shih-i 十翼
Shih t'ung 史通
Shu ching 書經
Shu chuan 書傳
Shu Lin-chang so-k'an ssu-tzu hou 書臨漳所刊四子後
Ssu-k'u ch'üan-shu 四庫全書
Ssu-ma Kuang 司馬光 (Wen-kung 文公)
Ssu-ma Mai 司馬邁
Ssu-shu 四書
Ssu-shu huo-wen 四書或問
Ssu-tzu 四子
Su Ch'in 蘇秦
Su Tung-p'o 蘇東坡
Sun Fu 孫復
Sung hui-yao chi-kao 宋會要輯稿

Ta-hsueh 大學

Ta-hsueh chang-chü 大學章句

Ta-hsueh chang-chü hsu 大學章句序

Ta-hsueh chih tao tsai ming ming-te
　　大學之道在明明德

Ta-hsueh huo-wen 大學或問

ta-jen chih hsueh 大人之學

Ta Ts'ao Yuan-k'o 答曹元可

Tai Sheng 戴聖

T'ai-chi t'u-shuo 太極圖說

t'ai-ho 太和

t'ai-hsu 太虛

Tan Chu 啖助

T'an-kung 檀弓

tao-hsin 道心

Tao-hsueh 道學

tao-t'ung 道統

Ti-tzu chih 弟子職

t'iao-mu 條目

T'ien-sheng tz'u chin-shih 'Ta-hsueh'
　p'ien 天聖賜進士大學篇

Ts'ai Hsu-chai 蔡虛齋

Tseng Kung 曾鞏

Tseng Tzu 曾子

Tso Ch'iu-ming 左邱明

Tso chuan 左傳

tsu-k'ao lai ko 祖考來格

T'ung-an 同安

T'ung shu 通書

Tzu-chih t'ung-chien 資治通鑑

Tzu-lu 子路

Tzu-ssu 子思

tz'u 辭

wan-wu 萬物

Wang An-shih 王安石

Wang Kung-ch'en 王拱辰

Wang Kuo 王過

Wang Mou-hung 王懋竑

Wang Wen-cheng 王文正

Wang Yang-ming 王陽明

Wang Ying-lin 王應麟

wu 物

Wu-ching cheng-i 五經正義

wu-ching po-shih 五經博士

Yang Chu 楊朱

Yang Kuei-shan 楊龜山

Yang Liang 楊倞

Yin cheng 胤征

Ying Jen-chung 應仁仲

Yu Tso 游酢

yü 籲

Yü-hai 玉海

Yü-shan 玉山

Yü-shan chiang-i 玉山講義

Yuan tao 原道

Index

Harvard East Asian Monographs

STUDIES IN THE MODERNIZATION OF THE REPUBLIC OF KOREA: 1945–1975

90. Noel F. McGinn, Donald R. Snodgrass, Yung Bong Kim, Shin-Bok Kim, and Quee-Young Kim, *Education and Development in Korea*

91. Leroy P. Jones and Il SaKong, *Government, Business and Entrepreneurship in Economic Development: The Korean Case*

92. Edward S. Mason, Dwight H. Perkins, Kwang Suk Kim, David C. Cole, Mahn Je Kim, et al., *The Economic and Social Modernization of the Republic of Korea*

93. Robert Repetto, Tai Hwan Kwon, Son-Ung Kim, Dae Young Kim, John E. Sloboda, and Peter J. Donaldson, *Economic Development, Population Policy, and Demographic Transition in the Republic of Korea*

106. David C. Cole and Yung Chul Park, *Financial Development in Korea, 1945-1978*

107. Roy Bahl, Chuk Kyo Kim, and Chong Kee Park, *Public Finances during the Korean Modernization Process*

94. Parks M. Coble, *The Shanghai Capitalists and the Nationalist Government, 1927-1937*

95. Noriko Kamachi, *Reform in China: Huang Tsun-hsien and the Japanese Model*

96. Richard Wich, *Sino-Soviet Crisis Politics: A Study of Political Change and Communication*

97. Lillian M. Li, *China's Silk Trade: Traditional Industry in the Modern World, 1842-1937*

98. R. David Arkush, *Fei Xiaotong and Sociology in Revolutionary China*

99. Kenneth Alan Grossberg, *Japan's Renaissance: The Politics of the Muromachi Bakufu*

100. James Reeve Pusey, *China and Charles Darwin*

101. Hoyt Cleveland Tillman, *Utilitarian Confucianism: Ch'en Liang's Challenge to Chu Hsi*

102. Thomas A. Stanley, *Ōsugi Sakae, Anarchist in Taishō Japan: The Creativity of the Ego*

103. Jonathan K. Ocko, *Bureaucratic Reform in Provincial China: Ting Jih-ch'ang in Restoration Kiangsu, 1867-1870*

104. James Reed, *The Missionary Mind and American East Asia Policy, 1911-1915*

105. Neil L. Waters, *Japan's Local Pragmatists: The Transition from Bakumatsu to Meiji in the Kawasaki Region*

108. William D. Wray, *Mitsubishi and the N.Y.K., 1870-1914: Business Strategy in the Japanese Shipping Industry*

109. Ralph William Huenemann, *The Dragon and the Iron Horse: The Economics of Railroads in China, 1876-1937*